The Long Island Rail Road

IN EARLY PHOTOGRAPHS

BY

RON ZIEL

Dover Publications, Inc.
New York

*To the memory of the late Winfield Scott Boerckel, Jr., perhaps
the most knowledgeable operating official in Long Island Rail Road
history, as well as an L.I.R.R. historian and photographer who
always offered encouragement to those who treated his beloved
railroad fairly in their writings.*

ACKNOWLEDGMENTS

Primary thanks go to the various photographers who so generously
allowed their own work and their collections to be used in this book; they
are credited in the captions. Special thanks to Art Huneke for always
being available to answer critical questions on short notice, and to
Charles Feyh, for supplying the Irving Solomon photographs.

Published in Canada by General Publishing Company, Ltd., 30 Lesmill Road,
Don Mills, Toronto, Ontario.
Published in the United Kingdom by Constable and Company, Ltd.

The Long Island Rail Road in Early Photographs is a new work, first
published by Dover Publications, Inc., in 1990.

Manufactured in the United States of America
Dover Publications, Inc., 31 East 2nd Street, Mineola, N.Y. 11501

Book design by Carol Belanger Grafton

Library of Congress Cataloging-in-Publication Data

Ziel, Ron, 1939–
  The Long Island Rail Road in early photographs / by Ron Ziel.
     p.   cm.
  ISBN 0-486-26301-0
  1. Long Island Rail Road Company. 2. Railroads—New York (State).
I. Title.
TF25.L6Z53 1990
385′.09747—dc20   89-25968
                                                                CIP

Contents

Introduction

OVER A CENTURY and a half ago—when the United States of America had been independent for just fifty-eight years—a special act of the New York State legislature chartered the Long Island Rail Road. The bill, enacted into law on April 24, 1834, granted a franchise to build a line from Brooklyn to Greenport, a distance of ninety-five miles. Its purpose was not to provide local service, but rather to be the southwesternmost link in a rail–boat–rail connection between New York and Boston. Coastal steamboats made the run in sixteen hours; the new route would cut that to just eleven hours. (Engineering wisdom of the day assured the promoters that it would be impossible to build a railway across the hills and rivers of southern Connecticut, seemingly guaranteeing the long-term success of the venture.) The line was opened on July 27, 1844, and was an immediate success. By 1850, however, the New York, New Haven & Hartford route was completed, creating an even faster and much more convenient all-rail journey. The very reason for the existence of the L.I.R.R. had come to an abrupt end; its fortunes plunged and it turned to scraping up whatever local business it could find.

Because the tracks had been laid right through the pine barrens in the middle of Long Island—purposely avoiding the populated areas along the north and south shores—patrons were hard to come by and the bypassed communities began supporting competing companies that were very willing to build railroad lines along the shorefronts. Sag Harbor is a case in point. Ever since the sudden demise of the whaling industry by 1850, that village had been actively promoting the idea of an L.I.R.R. branch to the South Fork that would bring industry and prosperity. For almost two decades, the railroad vacillated on the project, until East Enders were about to strike a deal with the rival South Side Railroad of Long Island to extend its tracks eastward from its terminus at Patchogue. To beat out this competition, the L.I.R.R. built a branchline from Manorville to Eastport and eastward to Bridgehampton in 1869, where it cut north to end at Sag Harbor. In 1876 the L.I.R.R. took over its rivals (there had been more than twenty separate companies on Long Island, all laying track every which way in a ruinous competition). By 1898, with the opening of the line to Port Washington, the Long Island Rail Road had reached its greatest extent.

The coming of the railroad to Long Island created an economic and social upheaval in the nineteenth century that was much greater than that caused by the automobile and the airplane in the twentieth century. In the early 1840s, the stagecoach trip from Brooklyn to Greenport took two and a half days; the first train made it in three and a half hours! Before the advent of train service (and this applied nationwide, indeed, worldwide), most people never traveled more than fifty miles from their place of birth. The average farmer or fisherman from eastern Long Island—if he could come up with the schooner or stage fare—could expect to make but two or three visits to New York in his lifetime. Cheap, fast rail service had ended the isolation of people, products, thought and culture. The flanged steel wheel on the iron rail, powered by steam, soon carried the Industrial Revolution to every sizable community and united diverse peoples into modern nations—especially the peoples of countries of vast wilderness and extensive frontiers, such as the United States, Canada and Russia.

The Long Island Rail Road also spawned the Island's tourist industry, which currently accounts for a half-billion dollars in annual revenues. Little wash-boiler locomotives carried city dwellers to Brighton Beach and the Rockaways in the 1860s; L.I.R.R. trains turned the railroad dock at Greenport into the gateway to Shelter Island; and it was no coincidence that the first hotel for tourists in the Hamptons—the Hallock House in Westhampton Beach—opened in 1869, the year the railroad arrived. In the twelve decades since, the L.I.R.R. has been in the forefront of bringing summer residents and tourists to the Island. Its parlor-car service, especially on the Montauk Branch, is still popular on summer weekends.

A century ago, the railroad handled not only practically all travelers to the villages it served, but virtually all freight, mail, express, livestock and other transportation. In 1898, the L.I.R.R. bought out the Montauk Steam Boat Company, and it operated the fleet of "white boats" until the mid-1920s. The year 1898 also saw the victorious American Army, after liberating Cuba from Spain, return fatigued and sickly to Camp Wyckoff at Montauk, where 25,000 soldiers were quarantined for yellow fever.

Many exciting and visionary schemes were proposed, some materializing, others failing. Among them was the nineteenth-century idea of L.I.R.R. President Austin Corbin to build an international deepwater port at Ford Pond Bay in Montauk. Had this plan succeeded—and it might well have, had Corbin not been killed in a carriage accident in 1896—Montauk would now be a huge port and the entire East End would probably be heavily industrialized and populated. Since World War II, the L.I.R.R. has retrenched further, relinquishing its former transportation monopoly to highway traffic. As late as 1953, a single steam locomotive was known to haul as many as 110 carloads of potatoes from the North Fork to Queens; now it all goes by truck. For over a century, when the growth of Long Island was determined by the railroad, that growth was orderly and manageable, even after the opening of Pennsylvania Station in mid-Manhattan and the direct access to Long Island via the East River tunnels in 1910. Now that road transport dominates, "the Blessed Isle"—as Long Islanders proudly referred to their home long ago—has been overcome by cheap tract housing, clogged highways, pollution, overpopulation and crass ugliness over too much of its 115-mile length. The railroad gave up express and less-than-carload (l.c.l.) freight in the early 1960s, the last mail-hauling contract in 1965. The Main Line freight now terminates at Southold, the Montauk freight at Bridgehampton; each now seldom consists of more than a half-dozen cars of lumber and chemical fertilizers.

The romance of the L.I.R.R. that so captivated the imagination of generations past has also largely disappeared. The last steamboat was sold after the 1927 season; steam and electric locomotives went in 1955. Most of the quaint Victorian depot buildings were demolished in the ensuing decade, some to be replaced by drab, utilitarian metal sheds, others to be abandoned, leaving no trace of the fact that trains once stopped there to bring people to new homes or vacation playgrounds, or to carry them off to daily jobs or to wars from which some were never to return. Today's Long Island Rail Road presents an image of high-technology efficiency, with shining stainless-steel multiple-unit commuter electric trains and growling diesels—unfortunately stripped of personality and soul.

As the L.I.R.R. continues on into the second half of its second century, it will probably enjoy a resurgence; in recent years the tracks have been completely rebuilt out east, and electrification was extended to Ronkonkoma in 1988. Annual passenger totals are rising steadily, and after decades of actively discouraging freight business, the parent Metropolitan Transportation Authority is investing millions of dollars to get it back! Certainly the Long Island Rail Road—now the oldest railroad in the nation still operating under its original name and charter—faces a promising future out of sheer necessity, with the general public now in open revolt against the abuses perpetrated by the highway–industrial complex.

Many collections of L.I.R.R. historical photographs, public and private, large and small, on and off Long Island, have been studied by the author over the past quarter-century, and about 4,000 negatives—including hundreds of glass-plates dating to the 1890s—are now in the author's own archives, including many discarded by the railroad itself. Since railroads' engineering, motive-power and publicity departments have extensively utilized photography since the mid-1860s, there was once a vast repository of official L.I.R.R. plates. The fire that destroyed the company's Long Island City headquarters in 1902 is the probable explanation why not one official L.I.R.R. plate is known to survive prior to that date. Despite a disastrous "housecleaning" in 1958, in which President Thomas M. Goodfellow ordered 20,000 plates discarded, some survived, plus hundreds of prints. Beginning with George B. Brainard, the official photographer of the Brooklyn Union Gas Company, in the late 1870s, many professional photographers have turned their lenses on the railroad. By 1908, the first railway enthusiasts began taking pictures of trains, and less than a quarter-century later there were many such amateurs with quality cameras, shooting action photos. At this writing, many are still alive and, fortunately, most are generous in making their work available to those who appreciate their efforts. Most of the prints in this volume were made by the author in his own darkroom, when the original negatives were obtainable. In some cases, quality copy negatives proved almost as good.

Different formats were considered for presenting the material in this book. A trip down the railroad, branch by branch, was one possibility, as was the idea of running the photos chronologically. Finally, covering it by categories (locomotives, stations, people, boats, etc.) seemed the most appropriate. In the end, it was decided to adopt basically the latter system, modified somewhat by using the two former to lend coherence and logical sequence. While the ninety years from 1865 to 1955 are represented well, the bulk of the photographs were taken during the last thirty years of that span, since so many negatives survive from that era, including the vast majority of action train photos. Since the perfection of photography coincided with the rise of railroading, millions of pictures have been made of the railway scene. During most of the history of the Long Island Rail Road—sixty-six years as an independent company, followed by sixty-six years as a mere subdivision of the once great Pennsylvania Railroad, since which time it has been owned by the State of New York—it has been well photographed. Because so many pictures were made, an impressive number do survive, despite the terrible mortality owing to the heedlessness of ignorant officials and widows of photographers, and to the natural ravages of time.

RON ZIEL
Water Mill, New York
May 29, 1988

CHAPTER ONE

Nineteenth-Century Steam

1. L.I.R.R. train at the Howard House, April 1865. Just eight years prior to the time of this photograph, Phillip Howard Reid had built this structure at East New York (now part of Brooklyn), in Kings County, as a grain and feed store. When patrons of the Brooklyn & Jamaica Railroad (now the Atlantic Branch of the L.I.R.R.) began utilizing its porch as a waiting platform, Reid saw a more profitable use and converted it into an inn. Soon railroad conductors were calling out the stop as "Howard House, East New York." Thereafter, horsecar lines terminated there and summer trains to Rockaway Beach also boarded passengers in front of the hotel, all contributing to its success. In this, the oldest known surviving photograph of the Long Island Rail Road, a classic 4-4-0* "American"-type steam locomotive and its single coach have halted on the run from downtown Brooklyn to Jamaica. Mourning bunting, acknowledging the assassination of President Abraham Lincoln a week after the end of the Civil War in the early spring of 1865, is draped over the doorways of the Howard House. *(Harold Fagerberg collection.)*

*This numerical designation, which may be unfamiliar to some readers, is the standard way of describing the groupings of wheels on steam locomotives. The number "4-4-0" simply means that there are four wheels in front (including those on *both* sides of the engine), four next (the drivers) and none in back.

2

2. Brand-new locomotive *Northport*, January 1868. In 1867, the L.I.R.R. ordered two locomotives from McQueen (apparently a predecessor of the Schenectady Locomotive Works). Named *Woodbury* and *Northport* (the former for the first station and the latter for the eastern terminus on the new branch from Syosset, which was to open in April 1868), the little tank engines were delivered in January 1868, when this photograph was made at an unknown location—possibly at the factory, when they were brand-new. One other photo exists of this locomotive, taken in April 1886, just a year before the engine was taken off the L.I.R.R. roster. This copy, recently discovered by William Asadorian, was taken from an original print, the oldest known L.I.R.R. photo made directly from the original negative. *(The Queens Borough Public Library.)*

3. Contractor's construction train, Whitestone, 1868. While railroads have generally maintained their own crews for the upkeep and repairing of right-of-way and tracks, the basic construction was usually done by outside contractors, who often owned their own locomotives, dirt cars, steam shovels and other specialized equipment. In 1868, Conrad Poppenhusen, a wealthy German immigrant who was developing College Point, on the north shore of Queens County, financed the construction of a railroad to Whitestone. Here, the contractor's four-wheel dinky engine is shown paused with its train of side-dump dirt cars during the grading of the line. *(Fred Lightfoot collection.)*

4. L.I.R.R. engine no. 48, *Benjamin Hitchcock*, new at the factory, May 1874. The developing technology of the steam locomotive made it the jet airplane of the 1800s, and the companies that built the locomotives were justifiably proud of their handiwork. In addition to having formal builders' photo portraits taken for officials of the railroad to hang in their offices, the companies sometimes had informal plates taken with the workers and crewmen haphazardly posed on or about the engine. Here, at the Schenectady Locomotive Works (a division of the American Locomotive Company after the 1901 merger) in upstate New York, five men stand by a brand-new L.I.R.R. 4-4-0. In the early days, steam engines were named; by the time of the War Between the States they also received numbers. By the end of the nineteenth century, when tens of thousands of steamers chugged over the American landscape, the custom of naming them was dropped—to be revived periodically in special circumstances right up to the end of steam in the 1950s. Engine no. 48, merely numbered at the factory, was named *Benjamin Hitchcock*, after the real-estate entrepreneur who developed such communities as Corona, South Flushing, Winfield, Woodside and other villages in Queens. L.I.R.R. officials must have had a falling-out with Hitchcock, for just two years later, no. 48 was renamed *Port Jefferson!* In later years the engine was known simply as no. 12, then no. 512 at the time of her retirement, about 1905. *(Alco Historic Photos.)*

3

4

5

5. Rapid-transit engine at Long Island City, ca. 1886. By 1880, the L.I.R.R. was operating little tank engines between Brooklyn and Jamaica as often as every ten minutes during rush hours. The small eight-wheel locomotive did not have a separate tender, and, since it was equipped with a large oil headlight and cowcatcher at each end, there was no need to turn it at the end of its run; it merely ran around the two-to-six-car train and coupled onto the opposite end, running in reverse half the time. Although the rapid-transit engines were used mainly on the Brooklyn runs, they saw service on other West End branches. By 1900, they even got as far east as Sag Harbor, where they handled the two-car shuttle to the Montauk Branch junction five miles away, at Bridgehampton. The earliest electrification project, in 1905-06, ended their careers and virtually all were sold for scrap. *(Author's collection.)*

6. Main-line locomotive no. 53, Long Island City, ca. 1886. Locomotives of the 1870s and 1880s were quite small compared to those built at the turn of the century, and the Long Island Rail Road took advantage of their low-slung boilers by perching the crew's cab on top of the firebox, rather than behind it. While greatly improving the visibility of the crew—a safety plus, especially when switching or running in reverse—the practice did

nothing to assist the aesthetics of these engines! There was also one dangerous aspect. At high speeds the connecting rod between the driving wheels could work loose, and, in such an instance, it could fly up through the floor of the cab and cut the engineer or fireman in half. Here, the engineer stands in his commodious cab while a pair of young boys cavorts at the back of the tender. *(Author's collection.)*

7. Train time at Babylon, 1888. Flying white extra flags on its pilot beam, engine no. 73 is posed at the freight house east of the Babylon depot, with an 1860s-era baggage car on the adjoining track. White flags then indicated—as they do now—that the train was not a regularly scheduled timetable run. It could have been an excursion special, an inspection train for officials of the road, or even a photographer's train. Running photographer's trains was a common practice when railroads were the major publishers of guidebooks and promoters of local scenic and tourism sites. Since the collodion wet-plates of the day had to be developed immediately after being exposed, a darkroom was set up on the train, enabling the photographer and his assistants to coat the plates and process them on the spot. *(Author's collection.)*

8. Tank engine at Long Beach, 1888. In this photo, reproduced from a stereoscopic slide, tank engine no. 4 has already run around her train and is coupled nose-first to an open-vestibule coach, prior to the return trip to Jamaica. At this time, the Long Beach Branch was used only during the summer season. The L.I.R.R. presence turned Long Beach into a popular resort, with hotels, summer homes and, by the turn of the century, a growing year-round community. While the engineer lolls in the cab, the fireman stands on top of the boiler, polishing the gleaming brass bell. A boy wearing a straw hat stands on the platform, engrossed in studying the machinery that transmitted the energy of steam from the cylinders to the driving wheels. *(Author's collection.)*

9. Locomotive on the dunes, Long Beach, 1892. Around 1890, a prominent Long Island judge named John Work became an amateur photographer, recording scenes in Manhattan and the south shore of Queens County (part of which became Nassau County in 1898). Here he has captured an image of sleek engine no. 55, her engineer (second from right), fireman (far left), conductor (right) and two trainmen (wearing white hats) as the engine sits on a stretch of track laid right across the dunes near Long Beach. For less than a decade, ending in 1894, the tracks extended all the way east to Point Lookout. That portion was washed away by storms

each winter, so the railroad finally abandoned it beyond Long Beach station. The exact location of this photo is uncertain. If it is Point Lookout, this is the only known picture of this desolate stretch of track, which returned to the capriciousness of nature nearly a century ago. *(Author's collection.)*

10. Rapid-transit engine and crew, Rockaway Junction, 1904. The era of the steam-powered rapid-transit trains was drawing to a close when this engineer, his teenage fireboy and the conductor and trainman posed by engine no. 220 the year before the first electrification project was inaugurated. Rockaway Junction (now Hillside) was named for the simple fact that it was the junction where the New York & Rockaway Railroad joined the Main Line of the L.I.R.R. With the initial electrification from Brooklyn to Queens in 1905, about forty tank engines were consigned to scrap. Also during this period (1901–06) the railroad completely modernized its steam passenger fleet by purchasing seventy new high-speed locomotives, plus some new freight haulers, resulting in the retirement of all but the newest of nineteenth-century steam engines. During the first decade of the twentieth century, the L.I.R.R. evolved from a bucolic country line into the modern commuter conveyor it is today. *(The Queens Borough Public Library.)*

8

11. Wading River, ca. 1896. In 1895, visionary Long Island Rail Road President Austin Corbin extended the Port Jefferson Branch to Wading River and the Sag Harbor Branch from a junction at Bridgehampton all the way to Montauk. This rare photo shows engine no. 99, built by the Rogers Locomotive Works—the renowned creator of top-quality engines in Paterson, New Jersey—in 1886, and a dozen railroad men at the new Wading River station. Coupled to the tender is a most unusual car—an 1860s-era coach converted to work-train service with the addition of a caboose cupola. The Wading River Branch was abandoned in 1938. *(Author's collection.)*

12. Long Island Rail Road daycoach, 1877. Within a decade after the Civil War, with Long Island experiencing rapid growth, the railroad began investing in a third generation of passenger cars. Despite going into receivership the year following the mergers that saw the L.I.R.R. absorb its competitors in 1876, the enlightened regime of Conrad Poppenhusen and President Henry Havemeyer had greatly improved all facets of passenger and freight service. Jackson & Sharp, the renowned car builders of Wilmington, Delaware, constructed six new mainline coaches, painted cream, with ornate trim, in 1877. Although historical research inevitably produces contradictory evidence, it is believed that coach no. 3, shown here at the factory, was one of them. It is also possible that the low numbers were a public-relations ploy, to show off a new and reinvigorated L.I.R.R. under the new administration. These cars remained in service more than twenty years, ultimately winding up in such secondary services as those of the Sag Harbor Branch and the Amagansett-to-Greenport (via Manorville) local, known for over a half-century by the affectionate name of "The Scoot," or "The Cape Horn Train" (alluding to its semicircular routing). *(Jeffrey Winslow collection.)*

13. 1870s coaches at Long Beach, 1892. While Oliver Charlick was president of the L.I.R.R. (1863–75), he instituted a timid policy of running a small number of summer excursion trains to Long Island's seaside resorts—particularly the Rockaways. His successors immediately expanded the program with great vigor, and soon trainloads of sunseekers were bound not only for the beaches south of Jamaica Bay but for Long Beach and even Shelter Island—reached by a direct ferry connection from the original east-end terminal at Greenport. In addition to pressing every available main-line coach into service, the management began ordering open excursion cars, to be used only during the four-month summer season, in 1877. On July 15, 1877, to take an example of just one day, eighty-one cars, jam-packed with bathers, left Long Island City for Rockaway. Indeed, the railroad had drastically changed the lives of the common folk in just a generation. Here, in the summer of 1892, a coach and a combine (a combination baggage car and coach) await departure at Long Beach—possibly even at Point Lookout. *(Author's collection.)*

14. Dirt train on the Bay Ridge branch, Sept. 27, 1907. In a remarkable resemblance to the work that was going on in Panama at the same time, when the Canal Company was excavating Culebra Cut, a Long Island locomotive slowly moves dump cars as they are loaded by a massive steam shovel. The scene is in south Brooklyn. At this early date the L.I.R.R. was engaged in eliminating all of the grade crossings on its Bay Ridge Branch, raising the track in some places, depressing it in others. While Colonel Goethals had to contend with mud at Culebra, the L.I.R.R. was blasting through bedrock and glacial boulders in Brooklyn. Ten-wheeler no. 120, shown here, was built as no. 144 by the Baldwin Locomotive Works of Philadelphia in 1892 and survived in active service until 1925. Thirty-three years was a lifespan longer than that of most L.I.R.R. steam engines, few of which lasted thirty years before being replaced with more modern motive power. In an ironic twist, though the Bay Ridge Branch was transferred to the Pennsylvania Railroad when that company sold the L.I.R.R. to New York State in 1965, Conrail—the successor of the merged Pennsylvania and New York Central systems—sold it back to the Long Island Rail Road in the 1980s! Currently, L.I.R.R. management is considering ways of revitalizing the once-flourishing freight business on the line. *(Art Huneke collection.)*

15. Early Pennsylvania Railroad locomotive on Long Island, ca. 1905. When the Pennsylvania Railroad bought a controlling interest in the L.I.R.R. in 1900, it was for a far more important reason than merely taking over a small regional carrier of uncertain destiny. For years, the Pennsy had wanted to establish a huge terminal in mid-Manhattan, to rival the facilities enjoyed by its archenemy, the New York Central. While the P.R.R. possessed the financial and engineering resources to tunnel under the rivers

to New York, it lacked a franchise. The L.I.R.R., under the forward-looking Austin Corbin, had obtained such a franchise in the 1880s, but had no capital to do the work. When the Pennsy bought out the Long Island's stockholders, it also got the franchise, and within a decade the tunnels extended from New Jersey, under the Hudson River, to Manhattan Island and then under the East River to a linkup with the L.I.R.R. at Long Island City. For nearly three decades after acquiring the L.I.R.R., the P.R.R. allowed it an unusual amount of autonomy, but the influence of the new owner was bound to be felt. Ultimately, the Pennsylvania sold or leased to the L.I.R.R. nearly four hundred steam locomotives over a fifty-two-year period, beginning with the sale, in October 1903, of four early-1890s Consolidation (2–8–0) H-3 freight engines. These "beetlehounds"—as nicknamed by L.I.R.R. crews—were joined by seven more by 1905, and they became jack-of-all-trades freight movers over the next two decades. First used on main-line freights, they were soon downgraded to local freights and switching duties. Here a full crew of eight men (engineer, fireman, conductor and five brakemen) are seen posed with no. 166. Although L.I.R.R. trains were equipped with air brakes in the 1890s, they were not always reliable, sometimes requiring the engineer to whistle "down brakes," which would send the conductor and the brakemen scurrying to the tops of the cars with their clubs to tighten up the brake wheels to bring a train under control. Prior to the adoption of the Westinghouse air brake, just the steam brake on the engine and men "decorating the tops" of freight cars were used to halt a train—dangerous work, necessitating a large crew. *(Author's collection.)*

16

16. **The railroad on Atlantic Avenue, ca. 1897.** When the original Brooklyn & Jamaica line was built in the mid-1830s, its tracks traversed dirt roads and farmland for most of the ten-mile route. Within a few years however, the progress and prosperity sired by the railroad had created a major transportation artery, with Atlantic Avenue running along both sides of the right-of-way. Close proximity to the railway line was a prerequisite for the success of both residential and business development, yet by the mid-1850s a vociferous minority was demanding that steam power be banned from the Atlantic Avenue route. Incredibly, the antirailroad clique prevailed and in 1861 the steam trains were replaced by horsecars that were even slower than the stage-coaches which the railroad had supplanted a quarter-century earlier. The L.I.R.R. immediately relocated its main terminal to the East River at Long Island City. Brooklyn was never to regain its former importance, even after the severe commercial de-pression created by the ban forced the leaders of Brooklyn to beg the railroad to return its noisy, sooty steam locomotives. By the end of the century, even the railroad realized that its running down the main thoroughfare of such a populated area had become intolerable to all concerned, as this photograph so dramatically illustrates. Taken where Fifth Avenue crossed Atlantic Avenue and the L.I.R.R. , it shows how the train movements could block cross-traffic, with engine no. 85 on a switching move at the left and a Railway Post Office car in the foreground, left standing in the middle of the road. At right, another train heads eastbound toward Jamaica. The two sets of tracks in the foreground belonged to local trolley lines. At this time a joint government-railroad commission was recommending that the railroad be tunneled and elevated along Atlantic Avenue, a project that was to be carried out in stages, beginning in 1903. *(The Queens Borough Public Library.)*

17. **New York & Rockaway Beach Railroad engine racing along Atlantic Avenue, ca. 1896.** Speeding past residential tenements, a main-line train of four large wooden cars, hauled by a locomotive owned by the New York & Rockaway Beach Railroad, further illustrates the inconvenience and danger in-herent in high-speed steam operations along the Avenue. In addition to the longer-distance expresses, more than sixty rapid-transit trains covered the route. At night, when passenger traffic subsided, switch engines worked scores of industrial sidings, keeping local residents awake. The electrification and grade-crossing-elimination project resolved most of the problems. *(Author's collection.)*

18. **Superintendent Potter's inspection train at Ronkonkoma, 1897.** The turn of the century saw great progress in the moderniza-tion of the Long Island Rail Road, a circumstance due in no small part to the high caliber of its top management. Austin Corbin, who had ruled the line from 1880 until his accidental death in 1896, set a very high standard for his successors, all of whom were more than able to carry on the momentum he had begun. William H. Baldwin followed Corbin, and it was under his energetic leader-ship that the L.I.R.R. became part of the Pennsylvania Railroad and electrification was begun. He also laid the plans for the present Jamaica station and totally modernized the steam-loco-motive fleet. His able right hand was William F. Potter, whom Baldwin had brought to Long Island from the Pere Marquette Railroad in Michigan, making him General Superintendent on January 1, 1897. Also in 1897, the railroad hired Hal B. Fullerton, a renowned horticulturist, photographer and brilliant promoter, as Special Agent. When Potter ran one of his periodic inspection trains that year, Fullerton and his five-by-seven-inch glass-plate camera went along. For the photo shown here, Fullerton exposed a plate of Potter (second from left) and other officials posed with a gleaming engine no. 92 and business car no. 200, with the water tower and Ronkonkoma station in the background. After Bald-win's death, Superintendent Potter was appointed president on January 13, 1905, but within seven weeks he was struck by cerebrospinal meningitis and died on April 2. As genuinely popular as both Corbin and Baldwin had been, Potter was mourned by many prominent leaders in business and political affairs, as well as by all the employees of the railroad. He was succeeded by an extremely able Pennsylvania Railroad man—Ralph Peters—who was to rule the L.I.R.R. with foresight and grace for the next eighteen years. *(Photo by Hal B. Fullerton; author's collection.)*

17

18

19. American-type engine no. 28 at Greenport, ca. 1896. In the spring of 1893, Baldwin built thirteen 4-4-0 locomotives for the L.I.R.R. that were truly large for their time. With the accelerating growth of the company's business, the new engines went to work hauling long-distance passenger trains to Greenport, Sag Harbor and Port Jefferson. By 1895, they handled fast expresses along the new extensions to Wading River and Montauk. An engineer had to be held in high regard by the Superintendent of Motive Power to draw one of these large speedsters. Whenever a photographer appeared, the fireman was set to work wiping the engine, shining its bell and brass number-plate and then getting out of view so the engineer could pose proudly alongside his charge, as this dapper gentleman is doing at the compact terminal in Greenport. *(Author's collection.)*

20. Brooks locomotive and train at New Hyde Park, June 9, 1899. Built just fifteen months earlier as no. 33, 4-4-0 American no. 79 was renumbered when only a half-year old. Within two years after this photo was made, the Brooks Company of Dunkirk, New York, was amalgamated into the American Locomotive Company, but the L.I.R.R. continued to purchase steam engines from Brooks until as late as 1917. Here a nine-car train of wooden equipment, all clean and shiny and flying extra flags, has paused for Fullerton's camera in the fields of New Hyde Park on the double-track Main Line. In the closing years of the nineteenth century there was not one house in sight! *(Photo by Hal B. Fullerton; author's collection.)*

21. Interior of hospital car, 1901. In 1898, the railroad converted old coach no. 117 into a mobile hospital, divided into two sections; a completely equipped operating room and a "transportation room," with beds, stretchers, folding chairs and hammocks to carry injured victims. The car was under the jurisdiction of Dr. Valentine, the head surgeon of the railroad; presumably it was used at train-wreck sites and was probably rushed out to nonrailroad mishaps, such as fires, explosions or other calamitous occurrences resulting in mass casualties. This is one of only about four known photos of the interior of L.I.R.R. wooden cars and is interesting for the designs in the woodwork, the Pintsch gas lamps and the window shades. In regular service, the car had red or green plush reversible seats, varnished natural wood and, in the case of parlor cars, revolving seats and shining cuspidors. The last L.I.R.R. wooden passenger cars were built in 1901 and all were retired by 1927—giving the Long Island the distinction of being the first railway in the world to operate an all-steel passenger fleet. *(Photo by Hal B. Fullerton; author's collection.)*

22

22. Camelback engine and crew at Islip, ca. 1900. The burning of anthracite coal greatly reduced soot and cinders, but required an unusually shallow and wide firebed to make steam. In order to improve the engineers' visibility, the cab was moved forward, straddling the boiler and leaving the fireman isolated on the rear deck. Camelbacks (also commonly called "Mother Hubbards") were widespread in the Northeastern states after the 1880s, and, by 1903, one-third of Long Island locomotives were of the center-cab variety. All were built new for the L.I.R.R. in the 1898–1903 period, except nos. 43–63, which were rebuilt from older standard engines, and nos. 198–200, purchased secondhand from the Pennsylvania. With the engineer provided only two feet of space between the boiler and the cab wall, and the fireman shoveling on the wind-blown fire deck, it was said that "in the summer the engineer roasted and in the winter the fireman froze." The separation of the two enginemen was also dangerous, since they could not acknowledge signal aspects or alert each other to other dangers. Instances occurred of the engineer suffering a heart attack or stroke at the throttle and the fireman being unaware until the train sped through the next station stop at sixty miles per hour! The last L.I.R.R. camelback was retired in 1931. *(John Jett collection.)*

23. The old and the new: Sunnyside Yard, December 4, 1910. The first L.I.R.R. electric train ran out of Pennsylvania Station in Manhattan on September 8, 1910, inaugurating the modern age of mass transportation on Long Island. The L.I.R.R. continued to dispatch steam trains from Long Island City for the next forty-five years and still runs diesels out of that terminal. Here, sleek little 1890s camelback no. 58 sprints along with a three-car consist of wooden cars, probably bound for Port Washington, the branch to which was not electrified until October 1913. That project and the contemporary electrification of the Whitestone Branch provided for the retirement of more than a score of steam engines, and, by 1917, all twenty-one (nos. 43–63) of these little camelbacks were scrapped. The passing age, represented by no. 58 and wooden cars, was contrasted by the newly electrified trackage on which she ran (note the third rail), the electric semaphores above her and the vast new Sunnyside Yard at the right. *(Photo by Charles B. Chaney; Smithsonian Institution.)*

24. Coach no. 347, new at the factory, 1890s. Although an almost complete roster of L.I.R.R. passenger cars exists, those numbered in the 300s are a mystery as to their construction and retirement dates, but this builder's photo at the Jackson & Sharp plant in Wilmington, Delaware, shows them to have been typical of late-1890s construction. Finished in a dark color—probably similar to the tuscan red of the Pennsylvania Railroad—these cars, although ordinary day coaches, featured fine gold lettering and trim work. Heated by a steam line from the locomotive (as required by law since 1888, when coal stoves were banned in main-line service), the cars were illuminated by Pintsch gas lamps. Early in the twentieth century, they probably received electric lighting, ending the always-present fear of fire in case of a wreck. With the first electrification and the Federal requirement that wooden passenger cars could not use the tunnels to Brooklyn or Manhattan, the L.I.R.R. embarked on a program of steel-car construction. In addition to the threat of fire, many passengers were killed or severely injured in wrecks occurring at speeds above thirty miles per hour, when the cars violently shattered into splinters, impaling the riders inside. Except for the last wooden cars, built in 1902, they all had open vestibules. The safer closed ends were more aptly associated with steel construction. *(Author's collection.)*

25. Camelback engine on turntable, Morris Park, ca. 1900. In 1898, the Long Island took delivery of three large 2–8–0 camelbacks, nos. 151–153, designated class H-51. Nos. 154 and 155 were built five years later, and, at the time, they were the heaviest locomotives owned by the railroad. They worked main-line freights and later worked as yard switchers until their retirement (four in 1928, one lasting until 1930), when they were replaced by larger 1915-era engines from the Pennsy. *(Author's collection.)*

26. Engine no. 32 slides off Long Wharf, July 27, 1908. Engineer Joseph Smith was routinely switching two carloads of coal, destined for the boilers of the Montauk Steam Boat Company vessels tied up at Long Wharf, Sag Harbor, when the cribbing, fill, tracks, engine and tender slid down into the water. Fireman Edward Hubbard "joined the birds" (L.I.R.R. slang for jumping off a moving locomotive) but Smith, in the manner of a ship's captain, rode down with no. 32, an 1882 Rogers graduate. A few

years previously, the same engine had derailed on the wharf and more recently had pushed a coal car right off the end of the loading trestle. *(Author's collection.)*

27. Six-wheel switch engine at Morris Park, ca. 1915. Shunting locomotives, built for that purpose, are most recognizable by the absence of small nonpowered carrying wheels fore and aft. Working at slow speeds and moving heavy loads in yards, they do not require the additional trucks to guide them into curves, and carrying all the weight on their driving wheels gives them much-needed brute strength. No. 197 was one of thirty 0–6–0 switchers built between 1889 and 1913, mainly to shunt for the industries of Brooklyn and Queens and to assemble main-line freights bound for the eastern reaches of the railroad. Like most of her sisters, no. 197 was replaced by a larger, modern 0–8–0 in the 1920s. *(Author's collection.)*

28. Assembling freight trains, Holban Yard, ca. 1923. With the opening of the present Jamaica station, the main freight yard was moved a few miles east along the Main Line, to Hollis, where it remained until the early 1980s. Here, a turn-of-the-century camelback and a smaller six-wheel switcher with sloping tender (providing better visibility for the engine crew) move wooden boxcars over the many switches. With the precipitous drop in freight service, all classification is now performed at Long Island City. *(Photo by James V. Osborne; author's collection.)*

CHAPTER TWO

Historical Events and the Long Island Rail Road

29. Spanish-American War veterans disembarking at Montauk, August 1898. The Spanish-American War, which lasted little more than three months, was perhaps the greatest military bargain in history. Within that short span of time and with less than one thousand combat dead, the United States evolved from being a regional coastal nation to one of the top five world powers. In fact, it is doubtful that, after the war with Spain, had the U.S.A. gotten into a conflict with any of the other leading nations (England, France, Germany or Russia), America would have been defeated. As a direct result of the victories in the Caribbean Sea and the Philippines, coupled with the annexation of Hawaii that same year, the Pacific Ocean had become an American lake and the Caribbean an American pond. What took most countries a century, several wars and hundreds of thousands of casualties to accomplish, the United States had done in one exciting spring season! Racked with malaria and thought to be infected with yellow fever, the 25,000-man army that had captured Cuba and Puerto Rico was sent to a quarantine camp at the most desolate spot available on the entire east coast that was accessible by railroad and steamship—Montauk, at the far eastern end of Long Island. In this photo, troops just returned from the trenches at Santiago, Cuba, disembark at the Long Island Rail Road dock at Fort Pond Bay, Montauk. These troops were to spend the next six weeks in misery—recuperating in tents on the wind-blown, scorching sands of Montauk—as well as luxury, as the wealthy New York capitalists who were reaping enormous war profits dispatched their gourmet chefs and trainloads of the finest food, in the sincere belief that "nothing is too good for our brave boys." *(Photo by Hal B. Fullerton; Suffolk County Historical Society.)*

30. Sick and wounded soldiers on L.I.R.R. baggage wagon, August 1898. The yellow press of William Randolph Hearst and Joseph Pulitzer had, in large measure, been responsible for whipping the American populace into the frenzy that brought on the Spanish-American War. After Spain had been beaten, they turned their editorial venom on the Long Island Rail Road for its unpreparedness and its failure to supply the troops at Montauk, making conjectures about enormous profits that the L.I.R.R. was supposedly reaping from the War Department. The truth was that President Baldwin of the railroad had been given just five days' notice that the ships that had sailed from Santiago Harbor were bound for Montauk! In that short span, the L.I.R.R. sent hundreds of carpenters and trackmen to Montauk, built a large storage yard and warehouses and dispatched dozens of trainloads of supplies, which were in place as the first troopships landed. The final reckoning, two months later, proved that the railroad had hardly managed to break even for its heroic effort, as it had pressed every locomotive, every car and every man into a massive endeavor to complete its wartime mission, with an unmatched sense of duty and professionalism. While most of the soldiers arrived at the dock in Montauk directly from Cuba, others came into Long Island City. When Camp Wyckoff (named for a U.S. Army colonel killed in the Cuban campaign) at Montauk was evacuated in September, the entire force of men left by train for Long Island City, where they transferred to other railways for their journeys back home. Here, Long Island Rail Road baggagemen haul several recuperating veterans up the short incline from the ferry dock to the station at Long Island City. *(Photo by Hal B. Fullerton; Suffolk County Historical Society.)*

31. Cavalry troop at Southampton station, 1898. The original notes with this plate refer to "the Rough Riders at Southampton, 1899," which is impossible, since that famed unit—under the command of Colonel Theodore Roosevelt and officially designated the 1st U.S. Volunteer Cavalry Regiment—was disbanded in September 1898, after a mere 133 days since its activation. Also, these men are dressed in the blue uniforms of the regular Army—not the distinctive khaki uniforms with polka-dot bandannas that distinguished the 1st Volunteer Cavalry. More likely, this troop had been transported from Camp Wyckoff to Southampton—a distance of just twenty-seven miles—by train to participate in a local celebration associated with the war in 1898. *(Photo by Hal B. Fullerton; Suffolk County Historical Society.)*

32. Theodore Roosevelt campaigning for governor, Babylon, November 1898. While Commodore George Dewey's great victory over the Spanish fleet in Manila Bay was the decisive engagement of the Spanish-American War, it was Colonel Roosevelt's dramatic charge up San Juan Hill in Cuba that, with the passing of ninety years, stands out in the minds of most Americans. Roosevelt shrewdly capitalized on the adulation of his countrymen when he ran for governor of New York State a few months later. Although retired from active duty, he campaigned in clothing of a decidedly military cut that could not but continuously remind the admiring crowds of his recent exploits. After whistle-stopping all over the state, T. R. wound up his campaign, a few days before being elected, by touring Long Island, where he gave speeches in major towns, including Riverhead, Greenport, Patchogue and Babylon, from the rear vestibule of an L.I.R.R. coach. *(Photo by Hal B. Fullerton; Suffolk County Historical Society.)*

30

33

33. Laying plankway for "Mile-a-Minute" Murphy, June 1899. When the unimaginative and bureaucratic record of the Long Island Rail Road in the late twentieth century is considered, the imagination and daring of its management around the turn of the century seems almost impossible, but for contemporary photographs and press reports. Austin Corbin ran trains from Long Island City to Montauk—105 miles—in 106 minutes: over thirty percent *faster* than the fastest trains today! Trains arrived no more than a half-hour late during the severe blizzard of 1898, while today the railroad makes no attempt to run any trains at all in similar circumstances. Early in the twentieth century, the railroad led the fast-paced development of Long Island, while today it belatedly and anemically reacts to it. Perhaps the most dramatic example of the leadership role taken by the L.I.R.R. in the old days was the world-record bicycle run of Charles Murphy, a speed cyclist who expressed his desire to pedal at sixty miles per hour. Hearing Murphy speak at a meeting of the League of American Wheelmen—a leading biking organization of the era— Special Agent Fullerton challenged his bravado by putting the entire formidable resources of the railroad at his disposal. The plan was simple: a two-mile-long plankway would be laid along an arrow-straight stretch of the Central Branch south of Farming-dale, and a hood would be constructed on the rear of a coach to cut down wind resistance and create a slight vacuum. A locomotive would power the car; Murphy would furiously pedal behind, getting up to sixty-plus miles per hour in the first mile if he could, which would allow him to make his record dash the second mile. *(Photo by Hal B. Fullerton; Suffolk County Historical Society.)*

34. Photographers record the preparations, June 30, 1899. To make sure that Charles Murphy's bicycle run would make worldwide headlines, Hal Fullerton waged a media campaign more than a half-century before such a practice became commonplace. Fullerton exposed this dramatic plate of Murphy making last-minute adjustments while some of the photographers present focused their view cameras. Within moments, Fullerton and his camera were on board the coach, where the redoubtable Special

Agent supervised the epic—and very risky—affair. *(Photo by Hal B. Fullerton; Suffolk County Historical Society.)*

35. Preparing for the historic run of "Mile-a-Minute" Murphy, June 30, 1899. Coming just a year after the stupendous victory over Spain, the derring-do of Murphy (and the cooperation of the railroad) typified, on an individual and corporate basis, the supreme confidence with which an emerging world power faced the new century. This photo by Fullerton shows a preliminary test run; during the actual record dash, Fullerton knelt on the car platform, shouting encouragement to the cyclist. As Superintendent Potter wailed, "The poor man will be killed!" little engine no. 39 (not the same steam locomotive that survives today) accelerated toward Babylon with Murphy's eye fixed on a white-painted board centered in front of him. Much depended on the ability of the engineer to accelerate, then maintain the top speed and decelerate without a single lurch or jerky movement, even one of which could cause Murphy to collide with the car, or fall back into the turbulence a few feet behind. Either circumstance would probably have killed him; at best he would have been severely injured. As the one-car train neared the end of the plankway, the engineer blew the whistle frantically, and Fullerton and several other officials reached down and grasped Murphy, pulling him up into the coach. The cyclist had wrapped his legs around the bike, bringing it up with him to prevent its certain destruction. When it was over, the stopwatches recorded that Murphy had pedaled a mile in 57.8 seconds, or more than 62 miles per hour! Actually, the train had probably hit 70 during the peak of the dash. "Mile-a-Minute" Murphy had set a world record, covering himself and the L.I.R.R. with glory. He later went on to become the first motor-cycle policeman in Nassau County. At this time, the L.I.R.R. catered to the bicycle craze; indeed, one of Fullerton's first official acts in 1897 was to order six baggage cars specially rigged to transport bicycles. The railroad carried tens of thousands of cyclists a year, where they made good use of the advanced network of bicycle paths and improved roads on Long Island. *(Photo by Hal B. Fullerton; Suffolk County Historical Society.)*

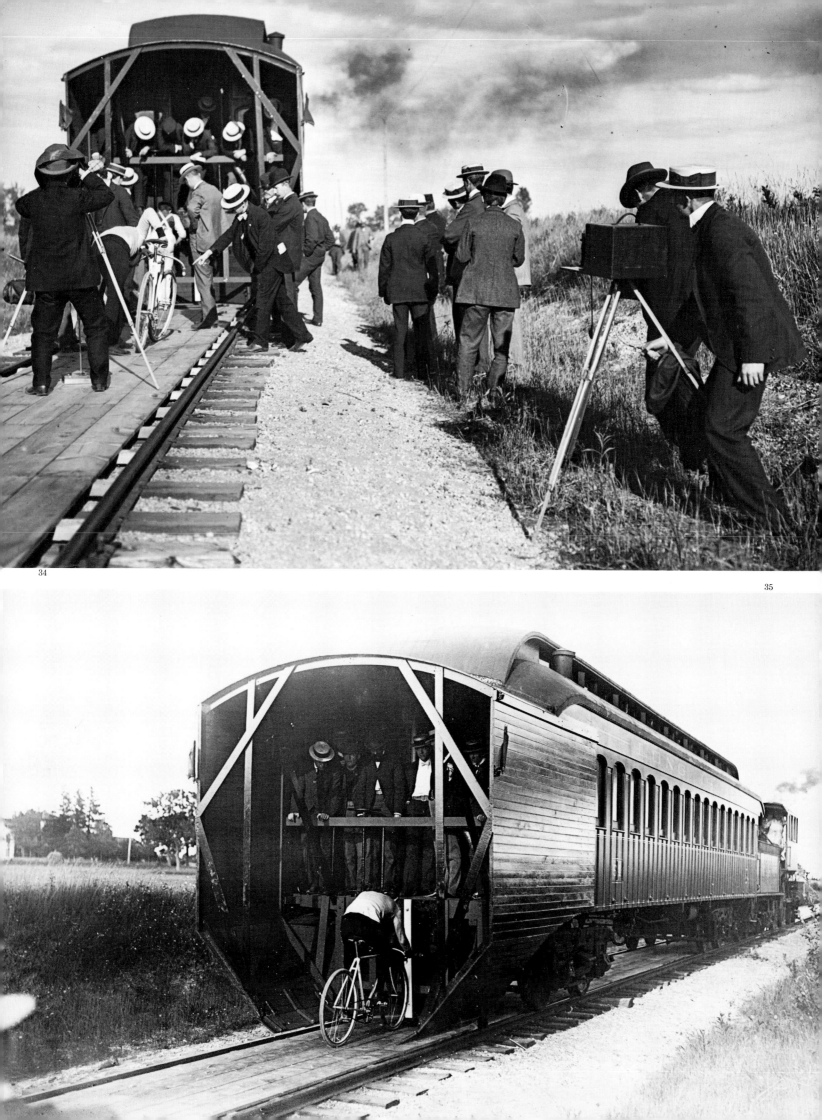

36. First connecting train from Penn Station, Central Islip, September 8, 1910. For thirty years, successive administrations of the Long Island Rail Road had dreamed of and planned for a direct route to mid-Manhattan, first via a tunnel from Brooklyn, then over the proposed Austin Corbin Bridge from Long Island City and finally by tunnel from the latter location. Eight years after the Pennsylvania Railroad had embarked on the construction of the Pennsylvania Tunnel & Terminal Railroad—which, at an astronomical cost of $125 million in 1910, was the most expensive private-enterprise engineering project of all time—the first trains rolled through the tunnels. It was a time of wild celebration on Long Island as crowds turned out all along the Montauk Branch, the Main Line and the Wading River Branch to welcome the first "tunnel trains." In reality, the first train of electric cars had disgorged its passengers at Jamaica, where they boarded old wooden coaches pulled by ordinary steam locomotives. What the flag-waving folks greeted at every bunting-bedecked Victorian depot on the railroad was a train exactly like those they had seen for their entire lives; perhaps only one-third of the passengers on board had begun their journey at Penn Station! Still, the celebration marked the recognition by Long Islanders that great change was coming. And come it did, its effects continuing right to this day as, every workday, the Long Island Rail Road still carries 100,000 commuters from their homes through the tunnels to New York City and back. *(David Keller collection.)*

37

39

-27-26
RR 214   THE WADING RIVER

28   *Historical Events*

37. First electric train to Babylon, May 20, 1925. In June 1924, the Long Island Rail Road's Board of Directors voted to electrify the Montauk Branch all the way from Jamaica to Babylon; just eleven months later, the first electric train made the run, ending in a tumultuous celebration. Compared to today, when years and millions of dollars in consulting fees are spent prior to initiating any such engineering project, the Babylon electrification, completed in so short a span of time and at an expense of just five million dollars, seems nothing short of miraculous indeed! Add to that the fact that the entire project—including erecting substations and high-tension lines, placing the third rail, installing a completely new signal system, altering station facilities and budgeting and allotting supplies and equipment—was done in-house, using only the railroad's existing work force and resources, without a single outside consultant involved, and the accomplishment is even more incredible! In terms of constant dollars, the recent electrification from Hicksville to Ronkonkoma cost almost twice as much for a shorter distance and took more than five years to complete. In this rare photo, scores of passengers wave from the first electric train as it nears Babylon station. *(Photo by James V. Osborne; author's collection.)*

38. "Electrification Celebration," Babylon, May 20, 1925. Thousands of people greeted the first electric train to pull into the new high-level platforms at Babylon, and the entire village was decked out in flags and bunting for the Electrification Celebration. A long parade stepped off from the flag-draped Babylon station, and, although steam locomotives still were to power many trains through the village for another three decades, the modern age of smooth, rapid electric service had made a spectacular debut. Real-estate development all along the newly electrified portion of the Montauk Branch boomed, and the commuter load increased dramatically. With electrification, the L.I.R.R. had no trouble absorbing the additional patronage. *(Photo by James V. Osborne; author's collection.)*

39. Engine no. 214 racing through Mineola, June 27, 1926. D-16sb 4-4-0 no. 214, one of thirty-one identical light passenger locomotives built for the L.I.R.R. at the Pennsylvania Railroad's Altoona, Pennsylvania, shops in 1905–06, had had a rather unremarkable career when this photo was made in the summer of 1926. She is shown pulling a train of wooden cars—equipment that would disappear from active service just a year later—bound for Wading River. At this time, third rail was being installed to Mineola. The new rail was in place, although the wooden protection boards were yet to be added. Less than seven weeks later, no. 214 careened into the history books and the folklore of Long Island. *(Photo by Charles B. Chaney; Smithsonian Institution.)*

40. Engine no. 214 at Calverton, August 15, 1926. On Friday, August 13, 1926, American-type no. 214, coupled in front of camelback 4-4-2 no. 2, split the siding switch leading to the Golden Pickle Works at Calverton while racing The Shelter Island Express to Greenport at seventy miles per hour. The lead engine rolled over on her side, while the larger camelback behind careened into the pickle factory with the Pullman parlor car *Easter Lily*, a combine and four coaches in tow. Pinned against the hot firebox by six tons of coal from the tender and horribly scalded by superheated steam from the ruptured injector pipes, engineer Squires and fireman Montgomery died in the pileup, as did four passengers in the parlor car. Here, the hapless no. 214, a shattered wreck, rests after being righted by the big cranes that the railroad maintained for just such emergencies. *(Author's collection.)*

41. Camelback no. 2 after demolishing the Golden Pickle Works, August 14, 1926. If no. 2 does not appear too seriously damaged after the wreck, it is because she had rolled over on her left side, tearing off the side of the cab, equipment and much of the boiler lagging. Here she is shown from the right side on the day after the disaster, after the cranes had set her upright but before they dragged her back onto the tracks. This photo—the most famous taken of what was to become known as "The Great Pickle Works Wreck"—clearly shows the tall seventy-six-inch driving wheels of the 1901 Baldwin 4-4-2 Atlantic-type locomotive, wheels that could propel no. 2 at speeds above 110 miles per hour.

The proud speed queen and sister no. 214 would never again know a hot fire or fast running; they were both towed to the scrap yard the day after this picture was made. *(Author's collection.)*

42. The destroyed pickle factory, Calverton, August 15, 1926. With Golden's giant pickle sign still mounted above the attic windows, the entire facility lay in ruins after the parlor car and combine had plunged right into the middle of the building. The four passengers killed all were in the first-class parlor car *Easter Lily.* One was Hamilton Fish, a prominent stockbroker, who died in terrible fashion: he was pinned under the wreckage, unable to move, and salt, slowly pouring from ruptured barrels in the factory attic, smothered him. Helpless rescuers, hearing his screams, were unable to reach Fish, but two men did get to another passenger in an identical predicament, and, by cupping their bare hands above the victim's face, they kept the salt away until more help arrived. A mother and her two young children were the other fatalities. The Great Pickle Works Wreck, which had claimed six lives, was a tragedy and the worst wreck in Suffolk County history, but there were at least four worse ones in L.I.R.R. history, including two in 1950 that killed 115 passengers and injured hundreds more. Nevertheless, in the intervening twenty-four years, the railroad carried over two billion passengers without a single fatality due to its negligence. *(Photo by Edith Young; author's collection.)*

CHAPTER THREE

Snow-Fighting Operations

43. Snowbound train, Queens, March 14, 1888. The blizzard of March 12–14, 1888, struck the entire Northeast with great fury and was centered directly over New York City. All of the area railroads were paralyzed by the drifts—some reaching heights of twenty feet—leaving thousands of passengers hungry and freezing on nearly a hundred stalled trains. The Long Island Rail Road suffered heavily in the storm—aptly described as a "white hurricane"—with two passenger trains stalled together at Queens (now Queens Village) for two days. Here, a snow-encrusted Rogers engine, built just five years previously, still has a head of steam as it awaits the arrival of a snowplow. The great blizzard of '88 prompted the eastern railroads to take a hard look at a new invention just being successfully adopted by the Rocky Mountain railroads—the Leslie brothers' patent steam rotary snowplow. A decade was to pass before the L.I.R.R. purchased a rotary, which was to prove the only really effective device ever invented for clearing tracks in heavy snow. *(The Queens Borough Public Library.)*

44

44. Snow-covered train at New Hyde Park, ca. 1899. Engine no. 29 (formerly no. 82, built by Rogers, 1882), pulls a lone combine through New Hyde Park after one of the severe turn-of-the-century snow storms, possibly the big blow of January 1899. Railroaders had contended with heavy snow since the earliest days, and it had long been an article of faith that neither effort nor expense was to be spared in keeping the lines open. In the 1890s, the L.I.R.R. maintained a fleet of wedge-shaped bucker plows, but in deep, wet snow, they stalled, even though pushed by as many as three locomotives. Although the railroad made heroic efforts to run trains, a really heavy snow could bring all operations to a halt. *(Author's collection.)*

45. Wreckage of triple-headed plow train, Queens, November 28, 1898. The big danger in using wedge plows was the very real threat of a sudden derailment, often with disastrous results, as occurred at Queens (Queens Village) during the early-season blizzard of November 28, 1898. When the plow derailed, catching fire and killing the operator, the trio of 4-4-0s pushing it also piled up. Derailments of the wood-constructed plows were caused by several factors. The operator had to know the location of every switch and grade crossing; if he forgot just one and failed to raise the flanger blades, the plow would wreck. Since the principle of the wedge plow was to buck the drifts at speed, snow that was heavy or deeper than anticipated could form a virtual wall, collapsing the plow against the force of the locomotives behind. As late as February 20, 1934, a plow derailed on account of ice in the flangeways of a grade crossing at Rockville Center (now usually spelled "Rockville Centre"), killing the operator and destroying the plow. Utilizing a coal stove for warmth, the plows frequently burned when wrecked, as was the case at Queens in 1898. *(Photo by Hal B. Fullerton; author's collection.)*

46. Plow derailment, Mineola, January 24, 1908. Wet snow is several times heavier than the powdery variety, as the crews of plow no. 2 and pusher engine no. 123 ruefully discovered while they were clearing the Main Line at Mineola. Here, the wrecking crane is positioned on the adjoining track to right the lopsided camelback and the derailed—but still upright—plow. Although the L.I.R.R. rotary was very active at this time, it could not handle all of the work, necessitating the continued use of the crude wedges. *(Photo by J. Burt; author's collection.)*

47. Italian laborers digging out as first train after blizzard arrives, Mineola, January 1899. In addition to utilizing locomotives and plows, the railroad would put many of its men to work after a storm, as well as hiring hundreds of local men and boys as snow shovelers. By the 1890s, the L.I.R.R. was tapping the spigot of Italian immigration by hiring many Italians for the more menial jobs of laborer, car cleaner, etc. The south Europeans soon began advancing in the company, despite overt discrimination, and by 1910 began filing the ranks of foremen and lower-echelon officialdom. By midcentury, second- and third-generation Italian-Americans had advanced to the higher ranks of management. The original negative envelope containing this plate actually had written on it—in Fullerton's own hand—"Dagos digging out"—using a word now nearly vanished as a derisive reference to Italian immigrants. *(Photo by Hal B. Fullerton; author's collection.)*

48. Triple-headed wedge plow, Peconic, ca. 1898. Keeping the Main Line and the Montauk Branch out east clear of snow was always a chore in places where few trees impeded the course of the winds across the potato fields and the tracks had often been laid in deep cuts. Here, the conductor and operator pose on top of plow no. 5, as the crews of the locomotives gather at the coach in back; probably it was meal time for the overworked railroaders. *(Photo by Josiah C. Case, DVS; author's collection.)*

49. Wedge plow in action, Mineola, Easter Sunday, 1915. When Long Islanders awoke on Easter Sunday, April 4, 1915, they found their routes to church blocked by a heavy, wet early-spring snowfall. The L.I.R.R. found its routes similarly clogged and set to work removing it. This view shows another shortcoming of the wedge plow; after clearing one track, the plow returned on the adjoining track, only to rebury the first one! The rotary, by contrast, expelled the snow for distances as far as a hundred feet. *(Photo by J. Burt; author's collection.)*

49

50

50. Two engines at peak of storm, Mineola, January 15, 1910. While the crewmen of a D-56 4–4–0 and camelback 4–6–0 no. 123 converse in their warm cabs, a derbied gentleman, his greatcoat whipped by the stinging wind, walks briskly along the fencerow in this dramatic photograph. Why these two locomotives are occupying the main tracks is unknown; probably they are waiting for a plow to clear some deep drifts ahead. Although the heat of steam in the boilers of these locomotives was measured in hundreds of degrees, the asbestos insulation beneath the thin sheet-metal outer shells retained it effectively, as illustrated by the unmelted snow pile on and around the boiler of the engine at left. *(Photo by J. Burt; author's collection.)*

51. The rotary on its maiden run, Bridgehampton, November 28, 1898. The Cooke Locomotive Works in Paterson, New Jersey, built the steam rotary snowplow and, in 1898, the L.I.R.R. ordered what was to be only the fifty-fifth one built since 1886. Numbered L.I. no. 193, it arrived on Long Island in November—just in time for the heaviest early blizzard in local history! Normally, railroad men loathe heavy snow, but this time the operating department must have been eager to test its new weapon! And test it they did, even running side-by-side clearing operations with a wedge plow on the Main Line in Nassau County, as a comparison study. In his capacity as Special Agent, Fullerton rode the rotary on its first two trips that winter and shot almost twenty five-by-seven-inch glass-plate negatives of it in action. This one shows an interested official (apparently Superintendent Potter) studying its impressive progress as it clears snow eight feet deep in one of the cuts west of Bridgehampton, on the Montauk Branch. The big oil headlight mounted on the hood didn't last beyond the first day's operation; probably it was smashed by a drift taller than the

nine-foot, eight-inch diameter of the spinning steel blades of the fan. On all of the plates shot by Fullerton on the second time the rotary ran—in January 1899—it was minus the headlight. After 1920, an electric headlight was mounted just ahead of the vent on the roof, a safer location. *(Photo by Hal B. Fullerton; author's collection.)*

52. Bridge Lane, Peconic, after the rotary went by, January 1899. Few photographs more strikingly illustrate the power of the steam rotary than this one, showing the remains of a fifteen-foot drift, taken by Fullerton just after no. 193 barreled through. A wedge plow, even if pushed by four engines, would have had to make repeated runs at this drift and even then it would probably have stalled—or worse. The pole with the leather thongs suspended from the crossarm was known as a "telltale"; it warned brakemen walking the tops of cars to duck because of the bridge ahead. The rotary was to outlive every other piece of L.I.R.R. steam-powered equipment, remaining in active service well into the 1960s. Finally, when it was to be scrapped, the author and George H. Foster purchased this last remaining relic of the nineteenth-century L.I.R.R. After trying for over twenty years to establish a museum of railroad history on Long Island to house the rotary and countless other artifacts, to no avail, the owners reluctantly sold it to Steamtown, the National Railroad Museum, at Scranton, Pennsylvania, where it is to be restored to its early Long Island livery. In reality, the L.I.R.R. should never have retired the rotary. Since its retirement, the performance of the railroad during heavy snowstorms bears out the contention of critics that, once the State of New York took over the railroad, it no longer cared much about serving the public beyond the barest minimum. *(Photo by Hal B. Fullerton; author's collection.)*

51

52

53. Marooned crewmen welcome rescue train, Calverton, February 13, 1926. The blizzard of February 1926 was the worst since that of '88 and, despite the constant running of engine plows, wedge plows and the rotary, parts of the railroad came to a halt. A passenger train pulled by engine no. 91 was stalled at Calverton for a day until 4-4-0 no. 205, 4-6-0 no. 137 and 2-8-0 no. 308, coupled together, broke through. The photo shows the elated engineer and fireman of the marooned no. 91 dancing through the snow upon the arrival of the relief train. Winter railroading on Long Island over the past century and a half has produced many a story passed down through the generations of railroad men and interested historians. *(Author's collection.)*

54. Locomotive-mounted wedge plow, Mattituck, February 20, 1934. Right up until the early 1950s the L.I.R.R. would hold about a half-dozen steam engines in reserve each winter with big plows mounted directly on the front. They were an effective means

of bucking moderate drifts (up to about six feet) and were less apt to derail than the much lighter plows. Heavy coil springs above the plow absorbed shocks created by hitting heavy snow or rocks, or such alien objects as cows or automobiles. *(Author's collection.)*

55. Steam rescues electric, Baldwin, December 27, 1947. Second in ferocity only to the blizzard of 1888, the one that began on Christmas Day of 1947 tied up most of the railroad for a very unlikely reason: just as the plows were to leave the terminal at Morris Park, a train hit a gasoline truck on the Main Line in Nassau County, halting operations for hours and burying the railroad. The press unfairly lambasted the L.I.R.R. for its "unpreparedness," and many trains loaded with passengers became snowbound. Here, a lumbering H-10s freight steamer pulls out the first of five multiple-unit electric trains that were stuck between Rockville Centre and Baldwin through a long, cold night. *(Author's collection.)*

CHAPTER FOUR
Early-Twentieth-Century Trains

56. Westbound passenger train, Mineola, 1909.
The bridge that carries Mineola Boulevard over the
Long Island Rail Road's Main Line has been a
favorite spot for photographers ever since it was
first built in 1880, when G. B. Brainard set up his
collodion wet-plate camera to get a high-angle view
of Mineola station. Nearly three decades later, a
young lensman named Joseph Burt took one of his
earliest photos from the identical location. It shows
D-16b locomotive no. 219 on an autumn morning
during a brief station stop. While young ladies in
"Gibson Girl" attire stand on both platforms,
another photographer has set up his tripod in the
shadow by the depot building at the right. Across
Front Street, at the far left, an automobilist is
cranking up his engine while a bicyclist pedals past
a second early horseless carriage parked behind. Joe
Burt was to live in Mineola for another six decades,
during which he became one of the finest photographic chronologers of the Long Island scene.
(Photo by J. Burt; author's collection.)

59

57. **Freight yard, Glen Cove, June 2, 1903.** In the early years of the twentieth century the L.I.R.R. carried an astronomical amount of freight, and virtually every station boasted an adjacent team yard full of interchange cars from railroads all over the country and Canada (and on occasion, Mexico), unloading all manner of cargo into horse-drawn wagons. Here, in the Glen Cove yard, at least twenty-eight boxcars, flatcars and gondolas have been spotted for unloading. As if this were not enough capacity, the men and carts at right were leveling more ground to add even more sidings. At the time, the railroad handled upwards of 250,000 freight cars annually, bringing in virtually everything used by the householders, industry, institutions and farmers of the Island, while carrying out vast amounts of agricultural produce, seafood, manufactured goods and sand. Cars readily identifiable in this photo represent such important railroads as the New York Central & Hudson River, the Central Railroad of New Jersey, the Lehigh Valley, the Erie, the Maine Central, the Chesapeake & Ohio, the Southern and the L.I.R.R. itself, which owned over a thousand interchange cars at this time. Ironically, all of those railroads have since lost their identity through mergers and abandonment—except the smallest and most confined of all, the little Long Island Rail Road! As late as 1966, the L.I.R.R. still handled over 100,000 freight cars a year; this bottomed out to a minuscule 18,000 in 1985—even as tractor-trailer trucks have continued to intimidate every automobile driver on the traffic-choked and pollution-spewing Long Island Expressway, Sunrise Highway and most other main roads. The freight yard in this photo is long gone, as is all freight service on the Oyster Bay Branch, but the Glen Street station, whose pinnacled roof rises above the boxcards, still stands. *(W. A. Boerckel collection.)*

58. **Engine and caboose of Speonk freight in Patchogue Yard, 1915.** Although the L.I.R.R. ran little four-wheel cabooses for decades, very few photographs of them survive. One shows H-3 "beetlehound" no. 163 and the crew of the local freight to Speonk posed on wood bobber no. 13 as they were switching the Patchogue

team yard in 1915. The gentleman sitting on the near platform of the caboose is conductor Raymond Robinson, Sr., who spent his life on the railroad, retiring in the 1960s. *(Author's collection.)*

59. **World War I troop train at Sunnyside, September 27, 1917.** Even before the entry of the United States into World War I in April 1917, a huge training base was established at Camp Upton, north of Yaphank in the midst of the desolate pine barrens in the center of Long Island. Here, hundreds of thousands of doughboys were processed before being shipped to the trenches in France, all of their movements to and from the camp handled by the L.I.R.R. Some of the most legendary runs of steel-nerved Long Island enginemen were made on troop trains from Camp Upton to the East River, where transport ships were waiting. Speeds of over 100 miles per hour became common—indeed, routine—as ships waited for the last contingents of troops prior to forming up in convoys for the dash across the North Atlantic Ocean. Little D-56 4-4-0s, such as no. 94, shown here bringing in the ten wooden coaches that formed the fourth section of the movement of the 69th New York Regiment, attained phenomenal speeds, despite their relatively low sixty-eight-inch driving wheels. The late conductor Harrison Moore related his experiences of riding the engine cab during a dash in which the train covered the fifty-nine miles from Upton to Long Island City in just fifty minutes. "I lost my lanterns and everything else on that run," Moore said almost a half-century later, adding that on some straight stretches along the Main Line in central Suffolk, the train was approaching 120 m.p.h. Hiram Wyckoff, who was to live on into his nineties, recalled how the post commander, General Bell, gave him and the rest of the train crew a box of cigars after Wyckoff had averaged 108 m.p.h. in carrying the general and his staff from Ronkonkoma to the camp. As it had in the Spanish-American War, twenty years earlier, the Long Island Rail Road covered itself with glory serving the nation during the First World War. *(Photo by Chaney; Smithsonian Institution.)*

60. Local freight at Bayport, ca. 1927. After switching the team yard and local sidings, the engine of a westbound freight has coupled back onto its train on the passing track. The engineer has just gotten a proceed signal on the semaphore down at the far switch, as another westbound train—reduced in the photo to the barest speck and puff of steam a mile down the main track—heads for the horizon. In a few moments, the freight will roll out onto the main and deliver the boxcars and empty coal hoppers to Holban Yard in Hollis. *(Photo by James V. Osborne; author's collection.)*

61. Speed queen engine no. 3 dashes through Mineola, July 10, 1926. Of all the fast passenger locomotives operated by the Long Island Rail Road, none were more renowned locally than the quintet of seventy-six-inch-drivered E-51 camelback 4–4–2 Atlantics built by Baldwin in 1901. Many of the legendary exploits of L.I.R.R. enginemen were performed while running engines nos. 1–4 as they sped into the folklore of Long Island during the first three decades of the twentieth century. Topping one hundred miles per hour when making up lost time or carrying prominent personalities in special trains, these locomotives, always requiring engineers with long experience and nerves of cold steel, were invariably run by the senior men on the roster. All four engines were retired by 1929, no. 2 having made her exit (see photo no. 41, above) in unusually spectacular fashion in 1926. As built, the E-51 locomotives could whip along a half-dozen wood coaches at ninety-

plus, but with the advent of heavier steel cars they were extensively rebuilt, and, even in the twilight of their service, they could handle trains of three heavy Pullman parlor cars and six coaches (all steel), as no. 3 is doing here. Zipping train no. 208 to Greenport, no. 3 is doing well over sixty m.p.h., as is evident by the fact that, although the curtain shutter of the camera has stopped the action, the engine appears to be leaning into the task of pulling her five-hundred-ton train. *(Photo by Charles B. Chaney; Smithsonian Institution.)*

62. Sleek engine no. 8, speedster of lesser renown, Morris Park, June 18, 1915. Camelback 4–6–0s nos. 5–19, although contemporaries of nos. 1–4 and more numerous, never gained the acclaim of their sisters, although some of them were almost as fast and often held down the same schedules. These G-54a (seventy-two-inch driving wheels) and G-54b (sixty-eight-inch drivers) ten-wheelers were the real backbone of the motive-power pool; when trains grew too long and heavy for the more nimble 4–4–0s and 4–4–2s, they easily took over. No. 8 is shown here shortly after emerging from the Morris Park Shops (west of Jamaica, Queens), where she had been rebuilt with piston-valve cylinders and superheating steam units, which increased her efficiency and tractive effort by one-fourth. This broadside view illustrates how the wide Wootten firebox rode over the wheels rather than between them, as was normal for engines of the era. *(Author's collection.)*

63

63. **Brooklyn Ash Removal Company car, Bay Ridge branch, February 1, 1934.** Through much of American railway history, fleets of freight cars—usually of a specialized nature—have been owned by companies other than the railroads themselves. Examples include refrigerator cars, which were operated by the largest meat-packing firms, produce shippers and breweries; tank cars, run by major oil companies; and, on Long Island, a fleet of ash cars. Virtually lost in history and operated solely over Long Island Rail Road tracks by the L.I.R.R., the high-sided wood gondolas, over 100 of which were owned by the Brooklyn Ash Removal Company, were a unique phenomenon on the Island prior to World War II. In those days, thousands of houses and apartment buildings, as well as businesses and industries, were heated by coal fuel, resulting in tons of ashes being cleaned out of basements daily during cold-weather seasons. The ashes had to be disposed of, and there was a market for them as fill at Flushing Meadow Park, before it became the World's Fair site. The B.A.R.C. cars were filled at various ash dumps from New York City trucks, which unloaded their cargoes into gravity chutes. An L.I.R.R. locomotive then assembled the cars from the different dumps in Brooklyn and Queens and hauled the ash trains to the Meadow. Retired engineer Richie Harrison recalls that all the brakemen who worked the ash trains carried .38-caliber revolvers to fend off the huge, vicious rats that often boarded the cars at the dump sites. Since the trains left fine clouds of dust in their wake, the railroaders referred to them as the "Talcum Powder Express." By 1939 and the building of the great World's Fair, the mammoth fill project had been completed and the ash trains passed into history. The millions of people who visited the World's Fairs of 1939–40 and 1964-65 walked on ground made firm by the meanderings of the Talcum Powder Express. *(Photo by F. J. Weber; author's collection.)*

64. **The passing of the old order, Mineola, September 11, 1926.** By the mid-'20s, the end was in sight for the small early-1900s 4-4-0s and the wooden coaches they often hauled. Within a year after this photo of train no. 526 to Oyster Bay, powered by 1904 Baldwin American no. 99, was taken, the six cars were retired; the locomotive was to survive a little over two years. Much larger, more powerful 4-6-0s and hundreds of additional steel coaches were soon to arrive, writing *finis* to the turn-of-the-century rolling stock that had served long and well. *(Photo by Charles B. Chaney; Smithsonian Institution.)*

65. **Sporty yard goat at Baldwin, Philadelphia, 1913.** Beginning with *Ariel*, the Long Island Rail Road's first locomotive in 1835, the Baldwin Locomotive Works of Philadelphia built at least 112 new steam locomotives for the L.I.R.R. over the next seventy-eight years, the final example being a pair of deluxe little superheated, piston-valved B-53sb's, in 1913. The L.I.R.R. also acquired twenty-four Baldwin-built steamers secondhand from the Pennsy, including several H-10s 2-8-0s built as late as 1915, but little 0-6-0s nos. 170 (seen here) and 171 were the final Baldwin steamers that the L.I.R.R. purchased new. With the exception of its second diesel, built by Baldwin with Westinghouse electrical components in 1927, the railroad did not turn again to Baldwin for motive power until the late 1940s, when it purchased six diesel switchers from the Philadelphia builder. Less than eighteen years after they were built, the Pennsylvania Railroad ordered these advanced shunters cut up for scrap, to be replaced by surplus P.R.R. engines that were over a decade older and of a far less sophisticated design, lending credence to the allegations that the P.R.R. often milked the assets of the L.I.R.R., forcing its stepchild to accept inferior equipment. *(Author's collection.)*

66

66. Freight engine and caboose in snowstorm, Patchogue, ca. 1948. Few L.I.R.R. men thought to take cameras to work with them, but fortunately, in the late 1940s, a young brakeman named Robert B. Morgan did. Here, when he was working a local freight, he took a photo of his snow-encrusted "hack" (L.I.R.R. nickname for caboose) and H-10s locomotive as they cleared the main track for a westbound passenger train from Montauk. These N52-class cabooses were of a standard Pennsy design and served the Long Island for over a half-century, beginning in the 1910s. *(Photo by Robert B. Morgan; author's collection.)*

67. View from caboose, Corona, Queens, ca. 1952. The freight conductor and brakemen rode the caboose at the end of freight trains on American railroads for well over a hundred years, and it is only in the late twentieth century that the venerable institution of the little red caboose is going the way of the steam locomotive and the passenger train, as most railways phase them out of service. At lunchtime, the engine crew and head-end brakeman would join the others in their home away from home. If there was an overnight turnaround, the crew also slept there; today such crews are apt to be accommodated at the nearest Holiday Inn. Heat to warm the men and their food was supplied by a coal stove, and there was ample bunk space for sleeping. The conductor had a desk to keep his freight waybills, and light was supplied by kerosene lamps, although some enterprising crews rigged up electric lamps, which were plugged in at terminals. *(Photo by Irving Solomon; author's collection.)*

68. Freight conductor gives the "highball," Holban Yard, ca. 1954. A hand signal from the conductor on the caboose, relayed by brakemen along the train, gave the engineer his go-ahead in the days before crews were equipped with two-way radios. Once he gave the signal, the conductor and any other men in the hack would brace themselves as the engine drew out the slack in the train. In a one-hundred-car freight, the locomotive could move a hundred feet before the caboose got under way, and, when it did, there could be quite a strong jerk as the rear of the train finally got moving. In the era prior to World War I, most boxcars were fairly low, so that crewmen sitting in the cupola on top of the caboose could see over the tops of the cars, as well as along the sides, checking the train for hotboxes (smoking, overheated journals), dragging equipment, unstable cargo, etc., as the train went around curves. Although higher boxcars (such as the one ahead of the hack in this photo) blocked the view along the top, the more important sides of the train were still visible. Later caboose designs eliminated the cupola entirely, substituting bay windows on the sides. Holban Yard, west of Hollis between the Montauk Branch and the Main Line, was the L.I.R.R.'s main freight yard from 1906 until the early 1980s, when all freight classification was removed to Yard "A," Long Island City, and a vast new railroad-shop complex was erected at Holban Yard. *(Photo by Irving Solomon; author's collection.)*

CHAPTER FIVE

The Demonstration Farms

69

69. Italian land-clearers at their boxcar home, Wading River, 1905. Ever since 1850, when the Long Island Rail Road found that its original purpose—as a link in the most direct route from New York to Boston—had vanished, it had been trying, with some success, to lure settlers, farmers and industry to the pine barrens of Suffolk County. In 1905, L.I.R.R. Special Agent, photographer and horticulturist Hal B. Fullerton persuaded the new L.I.R.R. president, Ralph Peters, to allow him to establish an experimental farm to discover just what crops the sandy soil of the Island was capable of producing. He then purchased ten acres of the worst land he could find at Wading River, where he and his wife, Edith Loring Fullerton, set up Experimental Station No. 1, "Peace and Plenty," the first railroad farm. Soon, an old condemned boxcar was unloaded at the site to house a gang of more than twenty Italian immigrant laborers, who cleared the land of the ubiquitous scrub oak and pine, so it could be cultivated. In this photo, the workers have returned to eat lunch at what was to be, for a few weeks, their home. *(Photo by Hal B. Fullerton; Suffolk County Historical Society.)*

70. Site of Medford farm, 1907. With the initial success of Experimental Station No. 1 at Wading River, the Fullertons turned to the Main Line in uninhabited mid-Suffolk, where, two years later, they cleared eighty acres for "Prosperity Farm," near Medford. In this "View of the Homestead," Fullerton has lugged his eleven-by-fourteen-inch camera to the top of the brand-new

water tower to expose a plate of the site of Experimental Station No. 2, as it was being cleared. Over a period of twenty years the farms were an enormous success, as the Fullertons grew nearly a thousand varieties of produce, many of them prize winners at County and State Fairs. The Fullertons may have employed a bit of surreptitious assistance; several photos show low-sided gondola cars—the type used to carry manure and other fertilizers—spotted at sidings at the farms. Fertilizer notwithstanding, they kept detailed records, and soon agricultural experts from all over the world were visiting the demonstration farms, marveling at their production. *(Photo by Hal B. Fullerton; Suffolk County Historical Society.)*

71. First train to stop at Medford farm, 1907. Engine no. 94, flying extra flags and hauling a baggage car and two coaches, pauses on the Main Line at the farm for Fullerton's camera. Probably the train has brought out railroad and government officials and agriculturists—perhaps just farmers who were to be convinced of the desirability of the land—as the first year's crop was maturing. Fullerton's ability as a publicist was every bit as vital as his considerable horticultural expertise in making the L.I.R.R. farm projects such stunning successes. Perhaps the most significant result of the farming ventures was the establishment of the State Agricultural and Technical School at Farmingdale, a direct outcome of the farms and of Fullerton's knowledge and charm. *(Photo by Hal B. Fullerton; author's collection.)*

70

71

73

72. Hal Fullerton in boxcar office at farm, June 16, 1910. Old boxcars were useful as temporary buildings, and Fullerton utilized several of them at his demonstration-farm projects. This one, probably at the Medford farm, served as an administrative office during the summer of 1910. Here, Chief Clerk William Hartman discusses a document with the white-haired Fullerton, as two other clerks work inside the car. By this date, the renown of the experimental farms and the writings of the Fullertons had gained international acclaim, and the summer staff at the farms required more than just extra plowboys and other agricultural hands. *(Suffolk County Historical Society.)*

73. Tractor hauling equipment, Medford farm, ca. 1909. Here a gear-driven early internal-combustion tractor was tested, along with a steam tractor, as the Fullertons experimented not only with varieties of crops, but also with the best equipment to use in seeding, growing and harvesting them. Fullerton had spent years in Mexico working on agricultural studies, so it was logical that, in 1919, he took a leave of absence from the railroad to head a distinguished commission of American farm experts that went to France to ascertain the best methods of rehabilitating the war-ravaged agricultural economy. *(Photo by Hal B. Fullerton; Suffolk County Historical Society.)*

74. Unloading L.I.R.R. farm exhibit, Riverhead Fair, September 1907. Wherever the demonstration farms exhibited their produce, Fullerton could draw on rolling stock from the railroad to move his displays and fruits and vegetables. Here, a pair of 1870-era baggage cars are being unloaded for the Suffolk County Fair in Riverhead. The portable buildings and their exhibits traveled all over New York State on cars supplied by the railroad, winning numerous prizes and awards and showering the L.I.R.R. with much-deserved favorable publicity. *(Photo by Hal B. Fullerton; Suffolk County Historical Society.)*

75. Loading exhibit for New York State Fair, Medford, 1912. The epochal changes occurring daily in the lives of most Americans early in this century is dramatically illustrated by comparing this photo with the previous one. They were taken just five years apart, yet represent two different ages. The first shows a wagon pulled by a team of horses loading wooden railroad cars, while this one typifies the modern era, with an early internal-combustion pickup truck and a new steel baggage car, the likes of which were to survive in service almost to 1970. The sign, with its map of Long Island, had become the logo of the farm projects. *(Photo by Hal B. Fullerton; Suffolk County Historical Society.)*

76

76. Demonstration-farm cottage, County Fair, Riverhead, 1908. A simple little farmhouse with Victorian gingerbread decor was moved in sections to house Fullerton's displays and was always a crowd gatherer at the late-summer fairs. Since both farms were in Suffolk County, the big Riverhead Fair was always covered, and the experimental-farm exhibits were viewed by hundreds of thousands of fairgoers over two decades. Railway officials, including President Peters, often were present to meet with the public and proudly extol the many accomplishments of their dynamic and progressive company. Hal Fullerton retired as L.I.R.R. Director of Agriculture in 1927 and Edith took over the job, but, soon after, the Pennsylvania Railroad, ending the long autonomy of L.I.R.R. operations in 1928, closed down the program, rightfully asserting that all of its objectives had been long realized. Mrs. Fullerton died in 1931 and her husband followed in 1935, leaving behind a rich legacy of agricultural and economic accomplishments that continue to benefit Long Island and its railroad to this day. Fullerton also left a treasury of writings and

photographs whose interest extends far beyond the shorelines of the Island that benefited so much from the dynamic endeavors of this unique couple. *(Photo by Hal B. Fullerton; Suffolk County Historical Society.)*

77. Interior of farm exhibit, County Fair, Riverhead, ca. 1912. "Peace and Plenty" and "Prosperity" were the names Fullerton gave to his two railroad experimental farms, and the interior of the farm exhibit's portable cottage, seen here, amply displays the abundance he produced at each of the farms, year after bumper-harvest year. Fifty-pound pumpkins, radishes as big as baseballs, beets larger than a man's fist and rows of jellies and jams all testified to what indeed could be grown in the sandy soil of Long Island. Even the livestock and dairy-products production was impressive. After the Fullertons left the railroad, the company lost and would never regain its leadership role in all facets of the affairs of Long Island. *(Photo by Hal B. Fullerton; Suffolk County Historical Society.)*

CHAPTER SIX

Stations and Structures

78. Stairs to tracks, Flatbush Avenue, Brooklyn, June 30, 1931. Many a journey on the Long Island Rail Road for more than a century has commenced at the Flatbush Avenue terminal in downtown Brooklyn. When steam trains of the railroad regained entrance to Brooklyn after the ban of 1861, they no longer ended at the waterfront, but at a new station located at the junction of Atlantic and Flatbush Avenues. Although the original (1836) line between Brooklyn and Jamaica still carried many passengers and much freight, its importance had been eclipsed by the new line to Long Island City. Still, when electrification began, in 1905, it was on the Atlantic Branch, and a commodious and handsome new depot was erected as part of the historic project. The tracks were now below ground level and adjacent to the new Interborough Rapid Transit subway line to Manhattan, facilitating easy transfer of thousands of commuters during rush hours. Leaving the spacious waiting room, L.I.R.R. passengers sought out the proper stairway to reach the train they wanted; each was clearly marked by illuminated signs proclaiming the track number and the destination and departure time of the next train. *(Photo by F. J. Weber; author's collection.)*

79. "WT" tower, Woodhaven Junction, November 12, 1931. Continuing along the Atlantic Branch to Jamaica, local trains stopped at numerous rapid transit stations, the most important of which was Woodhaven Junction, where the Rockaway Beach Branch (originally the New York & Rockaway Beach Railroad) crossed, with stations on two levels. This two-story wooden tower controlled train movements over the busy junction and was used until the last of the Atlantic Branch was depressed in a tunnel beneath Atlantic Avenue just prior to the American entry into World War II. Although residents and businessmen along Atlantic Avenue had long been agitating for the grade elimination, the worst problem was the blocking of numerous cross streets, as here, at 97th Street (formerly Napier Avenue), whenever trains passed. *(Photo by F. J. Weber; author's collection.)*

80

80. Rapid-transit station, Autumn Avenue, ca. 1923. This scene is smack in the middle of Atlantic Avenue, allowing just one lane for road traffic on either side—sandwiched between the narrow wooden L.I.R.R. platforms and the curbing in front of the buildings along the street. Along much of the route, the railroad was four tracks wide, in other places just two tracks, sometimes with additional long sidings for local freight service. Most of the stations along here were quite similar, with wooden platforms and various sheds, although Woodhaven Junction and Morris Park also had larger standard depot buildings. Although the elimination project solved the most pressing problems of safety, crowding and noise, it had some undesirable effects as well. A short-sighted railroad-management decision ruled against moving the rapid-transit stations underground, so the much-patronized service was simply terminated in 1939, leaving just the Woodhaven and East New York stops. Moving the tracks below the surface also killed the local freight traffic of many industries, coal yards and other businesses in the area. *(Photo by James V. Osborne; author's collection.)*

81. Jamaica station, 1874. The depot at Jamaica looked no different than many a rural stop, such as Mattituck or Southamp-

ton, in the mid-1870s, except that it was double-track here. A short passing siding, perhaps two hundred yards long, with a small water tower at left and a few other sidings, complemented the passenger station and freight house in the foreground. After the merger of 1876, the nearby South Side Railroad depot was moved to a point just west of this station building and the railroad plant at Jamaica continued to grow, culminating with the opening of the present elaborate facilities in 1913. *(Photo by G. B. Brainard; Brooklyn Public Library.)*

82. Snowplow at New Hyde Park, ca. 1900. A boy stands by the freight house at the east end of the platform, watching as a brace of locomotives powers a westbound plow toward the station, probably after the blizzard of January 1899. The train-order signal in front of him informed engineers that the agent at the station had instructions from the dispatcher for them. A few feet beyond the signal is a mail crane of a design used right until the L.I.R.R. stopped carrying the mails in 1965. A heavy canvas mail sack was hung on the two projecting arms, to be snagged by a hook on a passing mail car at speeds up to seventy miles per hour. *(Author's collection.)*

83. Grand opening of new station, Mineola, September 1923. Draped with flags and bunting, a new station of the popular gambrel-roof style, with high platforms in anticipation of the electrification that was to reach Mineola three years later, opened in the summer of 1923. The station remains today, completely overwhelmed by the surrounding structures that long ago replaced the few frame houses in the background. This complex is just west of the Mineola Boulevard overpass; the original station (see photo no. 56) stood to the east, on the opposite side of the tracks. *(Photo by J. Burt; author's collection.)*

84. Freight house, Hicksville, May 3, 1909. Taken from the rear of a moving eastbound train the very month that the railroad began a major improvement of its facilities at Hicksville, including new station buildings, an enlarged freight yard and a double-track Main Line, this view shows typical activity around a country freight depot. Freight handlers stand on the platform, amidst crates, while a teamster urges his horses over the tracks. In the foreground, a "gandy dancer" (track worker), carrying a shovel, returns to his task, while piles of dirt behind the water column at left indicate where work has already begun on the new platform. *(Author's collection.)*

85. New station at Holtsville, May 13, 1912. From the 1860s until the 1920s the Long Island Rail Road erected an incredible number of passenger stations along its various branch lines. Often an adequate, but plain, depot was replaced after twenty or thirty years by a fancy Victorian gem. Fires—by accident or design—took a heavy toll, especially when a disgruntled patron, a former employee with a grudge, or a farmer whose hay field had been set afire by locomotive sparks, sought redress. If the L.I.R.R. declined to offer monetary recompense for its alleged misdeeds, the local station became an obvious and easy target for revenge. Usually of frame construction, depot buildings also fell victim to lightning, electrical short circuits and—as recently as January 1987 in the case of Plandome—lone spur-of-the-moment arsonists. Often a small building had been sufficient when the railroad was built, but with the rapid population growth sired by the L.I.R.R. itself, larger facilities were needed. This trim structure at Holtsville on the Main Line caught fire shortly after it was built; it was replaced by a similar building. *(The Queens Borough Public Library.)*

83

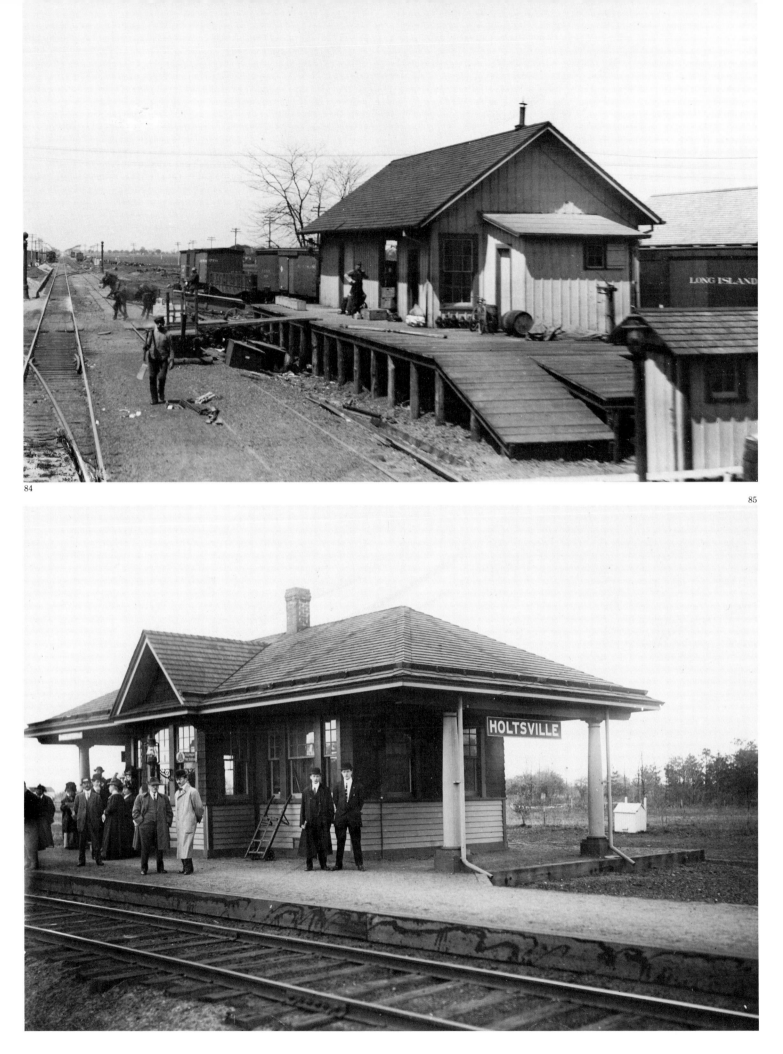

86

86. Yaphank station at night, October 15, 1952. Built in 1875 (with much more ornate gingerbread woodwork than survives in this photo), Yaphank was one of four depots of this quaint little design. (The others were Cutchogue, Cold Spring Harbor and New Hyde Park.) Utilizing the platform lamps and two fill-in flashbulbs for light, this unusual picture captures the lonely feeling of a country station in the middle of the pine barrens of Suffolk County in the hours after midnight. *(Photo by Robert Viken and Richard B. Wettereau.)*

87. Freight depot, Camp Upton, 1918. The hasty improvisation of wartime shows clearly in this picture of a portion of the railway facilities erected at Camp Upton, near Yaphank, where hundreds of thousands of doughboys were processed during the nineteen-month-long involvement of the United States in the First World War. Although the freight house is of standard design and appears well built, the platform is supported by tree trunks (probably cut from local scrub pine) which have not even been stripped of their bark. The open warehouses down the track are also of Spartan construction, while the track itself, hardly a year old, is bumpy and wavering, having been laid on a thin layer of cinders spread over tamped sandy soil. Expediency and lack of permanence are indicative of wartime waste, when conserving

resources becomes subordinate to military and political considerations. The railroad, which took the trouble to build the freight house itself to standard specifications, was proved correct in the long run. In 1921, the post was deactivated and 1,900 buildings sold. Since the L.I.R.R. owned this freight station, it was cut into sections, loaded onto flatcars and reassembled at Northport, where it served as the freight house for nearly a half century. *(Photo by Thomas R. Bayles; David Keller collection.)*

88. Opening day, Riverhead station, June 2, 1910. In 1909, the L.I.R.R. adopted the gambrel-roof style for many of its larger passenger depots, and for two decades it erected some fine examples of this aesthetically pleasing design. One of the smaller ones was the present station at Riverhead, the Suffolk County seat. Although its floor space was probably no larger than that of the 1870 frame structure it replaced, the first story was of brick and the canopies at both ends offered passengers more shelter from the weather than did the overhanging roof of its predecessor. This glass-plate photo is one of the few saved from about twenty thousand that were ordered discarded by L.I.R.R. President Thomas M. Goodfellow in 1958, destroying forever the visual history of much of the railroad during the 1902-46 period. *(Author's collection.)*

87

88

89. Depot at Jamesport, August 1879. After the Long Island Rail Road became a purely local line, its management realized that it would have to erect station buildings to serve the public and to house its agents. Lacking funds for such non-revenue-producing structures, the railroad, early in the 1850s, contracted with almost anybody who owned a modicum of a building near a stop along the right-of-way to provide a waiting area and to act as agent. As a result, Lakeland (Ronkonkoma) and Yaphank, as well as some of the seaside resorts, saw tickets for train travel sold in hotel lobbies. The original Holbrook depot was in a cigar factory, and the proprietor of a general store was the stationmaster and his porch the waiting area at Westbury. In some instances, a nearby private house even made do, but this station at Jamesport may well have been the most popular offbeat location among L.I.R.R. riders, especially when trains were late, for its main function was that of local saloon, offering railroad patrons a choice of methods of keeping warm! Perhaps as early as the date of this photo, it had been totally given over to railroad use; except for the addition of a bay window in the agent's office, its appearance changed little over the following sixty-five years. In 1944, it was extensively rebuilt in a nondescript cottage shape; it was finally demolished in 1963. *(Photo by George G. Brainard; Brooklyn Public Library.)*

90. Grade-crossing accident, Peconic, March 3, 1942. Less than three months after the Japanese attack on Pearl Harbor, an irreplaceable new Chevrolet sedan came up the loser in a right-of-way dispute with the westbound local freight from Greenport, pulled by leased Pennsylvania Railroad H-9s Consolidation no. 3468. Obviously no match for a 125-ton locomotive, the one-and-a-half-ton automobile was thrown ten yards from Peconic Lane and spun around, but landed upright on a switch. More than forty years later, when the author of this book was presenting his historical L.I.R.R. slide show in nearby Southold, he flashed this picture, wondering aloud if the driver had survived the altercation. "Hell, yes," piped a grizzled old voice in the dark, with a pronounced East End drawl, "an' she's still drivin' too!" On a more

somber note: despite a national campaign warning motorists against carelessness at railroad crossings and despite the fact that in the 1920s the L.I.R.R. had embarked on a massive grade-crossing-elimination program and was installing gates, flashing signals and watchmen at many other crossings, more than five hundred people lost their lives at grade crossings on Long Island in the 1935–45 decade alone. Peconic station was one of the earliest to lose its agency; already boarded up in this picture, it soon was to be demolished, to be replaced with an open shed for the convenience (?) of waiting passengers. That, too, was removed in the 1960s, leaving not a trace of evidence that trains once halted there, as today's diesels roar through at fifty miles per hour. *(Photo by C. H. Meredith; author's collection.)*

91. College Point station, ca. 1925. Conrad Poppenhusen had built the Flushing & North Side Railroad to serve his expanding development of the northern reaches of Queens County. While the Long Island Rail Road was frugal in matters of modernization and construction, Poppenhusen, who had successively taken over the Central and the South Side systems as well, spared no expense in maintaining excellent rights-of-way, modern equipment and substantial depot facilities. Headquartered at College Point, he made certain that the station there was impressive to all who came to do business with him or to purchase property. Two stories tall, with a mansard roof and a ridge-roofed center section, the brick structure was about a hundred feet long. Originally, it also had an attached shed covering the tracks, but that was removed early in the 1900s. By the time of this photo, taken less than a decade before the Whitestone Branch was abandoned, the line had been electrified and business was still brisk. The humped appearance of the platform roof overhang indicates where the train shed was removed. The great cost of eliminating the grade crossings led the railroad to choose the alternative in the 1930s: tearing up the entire branch. Foolishly, the City of New York ruled against taking over the line as part of the subway system, when offered it by the railroad. *(Photo by James V. Osborne; author's collection.)*

92. Night-trick operator, Locust Tower, September 25, 1952. One of the loneliest of railroad jobs is holding down the "graveyard shift" in the interlocking towers during the wee hours of the morning, when few train movements break the monotony. Yet the operator always has to be alert to work the levers controlling switches and signals or to hand up orders to passing train crews. Here the man at Locust Tower at Locust Valley on the Oyster Bay Branch puffs his pipe as he gazes at the train sheet. Surrounding him are the tools of his trade: control levers, scissors and daffodil telephones, signal indicators and clipboards of orders. *(Photo by Robert Viken and Richard B. Wettereau.)*

93. Platform shelter shed, Roslyn, October 18, 1938. Many middle-aged and senior residents of Long Island will recall commuting to private or parochial school via the L.I.R.R. during their teens, as this boy and the trio of girls behind him were doing over a half-century ago. Since the depot building stood on one side of the track, any station stop that had two or more main tracks also had a platform on the opposite side. To shelter waiting passengers, substantial wooden sheds were provided. Most were of this standard design, and few remain; the contemporary ones are constructed of steel and plastic. This particular one is still on site, now completely enclosed and used as a taxi office. *(Photo by F. J. Weber; author's collection.)*

94. Woodbury Road bridge, ca. 1880. Built in 1867, when the railroad extended its Syosset spur to Northport, this dubious-looking timber trestle was adequate to support the diminutive locomotives and wooden coaches of the era. Eventually, steel girders replaced the timbers, but the original brownstone abutments were to last even past the electrification of the line to Huntington, more than a century after they were built, not to be replaced until a road-widening project 115 years later. The basic dirt roads of the nineteenth century gave way to madacam in the early 1900s and more recently to major concrete arteries to move the ever-increasing automobile traffic. *(Photo by G. B. Brainard; Brooklyn Public Library.)*

94

95. Far Rockaway station, just before the rush, June 6, 1933. For nine months of the year, the sprawling depot facilities at Far Rockaway served as a normal outlying commuter and visitor station in electrified territory. From mid-June to mid-September, however, tens of thousands of beachgoers from Brooklyn, Queens, Manhattan and the Bronx would descend on the spot daily via the L.I.R.R., especially after the line was electrified in 1905. On July and August weekends the numbers of bathers could swell to astronomical totals, hence the unusually large platform shed in front of the station. Hammels, Seaside and Steeple-chase also sported large open-air shed roofs to protect up to several thousand people who might be waiting to board evening trains back to their sweltering tenements in the city. Later, this line was elevated, but the 1890 station survived on the ground until the late 1950s. The most direct route to Far Rockaway, via a long trestle across Jamaica Bay, was sold by the L.I.R.R. to the New York City Transit Authority after a succession of costly fires burned out large sections of the wooden span in the early 1950s. Now subway trains from the north and the L.I.R.R. electrics from the east both serve the Rockaway peninsula. *(Photo by F. J. Weber; author's collection.)*

96. Electric trains at Long Beach terminal, February 8, 1936. For decades, Long Beach was merely a summer-season operation—until the line was electrified in 1910. Prior to then, there were hardly a hundred daily commuters; within fifteen years, there were several thousand! A beautiful masonry depot with four terminal tracks and two long platform canopies, shown here with trains composed of standard Pennsylvania Railroad–designed MP-54 coaches, provided the capacity for the phenomenal growth of Long Beach. In the 1930s, the L.I.R.R. leased the land in front of the station, where stores were built right up against the once-grand structure. In more recent years, the stores were demolished and the station extensively renovated in a million-dollar project to restore the fine building. *(Photo by F. J. Weber; author's collection.)*

99

97. **Looking east at Ocean Avenue, Lynbrook, ca. 1906.** The railroad's official photographer set up the tripod of his eight-by-ten-inch glass-plate camera in the center of the eastbound Montauk Division track to get this view of a still largely rural Lynbrook, with the New York & Long Island Traction Company powerhouse and its coal trestle at right. The crossing—still a dirt road—is protected only by a diamond-shaped crossing warning sign with a bell box attached. A slight hill rises to the north, with wild shrubbery and weeds covering a vacant field. Down the tracks, other diamond signs guard other crossings and lower-quadrant semaphores govern train movements. *(Author's collection.)*

98. **Looking east at Ocean Avenue, Lynbrook, May 25, 1932.** Barely a quarter century after the previous photo was taken, Fred Weber, the L.I.R.R. legal photographer, set up the eight-by-ten-inch camera he used to expose sheet-film negatives at the same location, but on the westbound track. The changes during the interval are striking: the railroad had been electrified as far as Babylon in 1925, and Ocean Avenue, with the advent of wide-spread automobile use, has become a paved thoroughfare, which, in addition to the crossing sign, is now protected by a watchman (standing in the doorway of his shanty) who operates a set of gates. The New York & Long Island Traction powerhouse stands

abandoned, crumbling, with its lower windows boarded up and its coal siding long since removed. Down the track, position-light signals have replaced the semaphores. In the years following the time of this photo, the whole railroad was elevated through Lynbrook. The hill and field at left were leveled shortly after the 1906 photo was made. A siding—also equipped with a third rail—winds into the yard behind a building that looks older than its post-1906 construction date would indicate. *(Photo by F. J. Weber; author's collection.)*

99. **Brick station at Massapequa, December 16, 1930.** Built in 1892 and paid for by the Floyd-Jones family, the ivy-covered edifice at Massapequa, with its Gothic ornamentation in the eaves, was one of the most beautiful stations on the railroad. The freight house beyond it and the shelter shed on the other platform, plus the fence between the tracks, were typical of the station facilities along the Montauk Division at the time. Despite this being a weekday and the fact that Massapequa was well within commuting limits, no automobiles are visible at the depot, a sign that the Great Depression was settling in to throttle the American economy. When the railroad was elevated at Massapequa in 1953, this splendid station was demolished and replaced by an aesthetically catastrophic concrete affair, virtually identical with every other depot on the line. *(Photo by F. J. Weber; author's collection.)*

101

102

100. Wooden enginehouse, Babylon, May 16, 1918. In its bucolic years, prior to the Pennsylvania Railroad's taking over full operational control in 1928, the L.I.R.R., although extremely well run under a very progressive management, nevertheless had eccentric policies all its own. One such policy was to house its steam locomotives under cover as much as possible, resulting in substantial wooden enginehouses being built in villages where the tracks did not even terminate, such as Babylon, Patchogue and Amagansett. One-time terminals like Whitestone Landing, Locust Valley, Northport and Wading River also boasted frame enginehouses, while Bethpage, Greenport and Oyster Bay once had brick ones. When the P.R.R. took over, it demolished all of the engine sheds that survived (some had burned or been demolished earlier), including a large one at Long Island City, leaving just the biggest—a twenty-stall roundhouse—at Jamaica, the primary terminal. *(Art Huneke collection.)*

101. Original frame station, Bayport, 1902. Built in 1869, as the South Side Railroad of Long Island was extending its tracks from Islip to Patchogue, the small frame depot at Bayport was replaced just a year after this plate was exposed by a photographer from the railroad's Engineering Department. In the foreground, a heavy scale stands on the express platform, where crates of produce and barrels of shellfish fresh from the Great South Bay were weighed prior to being loaded into the cars bound for the markets of Brooklyn and New York. The new station, an impressive masonry affair, reflected the wealthy city clientele that summered at Bayport. In 1964, that edifice was demolished, to be replaced by a metal shed, which in turn was removed when the stop was stricken from the timetable in 1980. The nabobs had moved on to Fire Island and the Hamptons decades earlier. Today the trains roar through Bayport at sixty miles per hour. *(Author's collection.)*

102. Eastport nocturne, October 17, 1952. The frame depot at Eastport (called Moriches Station when the Long Island Rail Road ran its branch from Manorville to Sag Harbor in 1869, to prevent the rival South Side Railroad from beating it to the lucrative Moriches and Hamptons business) was typical of the circa-1870 stations, with its overhanging roof supported by diagonal brackets. In the days before rowdy hooligans began destroying everything not double-padlocked, surrounded by razor-wire concertinas or patrolled by armed guards, the L.I.R.R. felt quite safe in leaving a loose baggage cart standing outside and the door to the waiting room open long after the agent had gone home for the night. Most of the desolate little country stations of Suffolk County survived hardly more than a decade longer. Some were replaced by ugly concrete depots, others by exposed metal sheds, and some were abandoned entirely. *(Photo by Robert Viken and Richard B. Wettereau.)*

103. Station and shuttle-train platform, Bridgehampton, ca. 1923. Once the Montauk extension of the L.I.R.R. was opened in 1895, the five miles of track between Bridgehampton and Sag Harbor were relegated to secondary-branch-line status. Train service was maintained to Sag Harbor for the next forty-four years. Passengers were at first accommodated by a small steam locomotive and two wooden cars. In the mid-'20s a gasoline-powered railcar was substituted to carry mail express and passengers, connecting with every scheduled train stopping at Bridgehampton. The platform at the left stood between the Montauk Branch and Sag Harbor Branch tracks, and a tiny canopy offered a modicum of shelter for the patrons who had arrived from the old whaling port to catch a connecting train. The station, erected in 1884 after the original one had burned, was demolished eighty years later and replaced with a shed hardly bigger than that on the Sag Harbor Branch platform. *(Photo by James V. Osborne; author's collection.)*

104. Sag Harbor, end of the line, 1878. Opened just eight years prior to the time of this photograph, the terminal station of the Sag Harbor Branch was a modestly decorated Victorian building of equally modest dimensions, perched just beyond the end of the tracks, where it was to be a tempting target for runaway trains until the turn of the century. Indeed, on a foggy winter night in 1882, engineer James McMahon, Sr., mistook the lights of a steamboat tied up at Long Wharf for the home signal and ran engine no. 80 into the ground right alongside the depot structure. Had he been on one of the other pair of terminal tracks, McMahon would have demolished the station. Finally, in the late 1890s, the station was moved around to the south side of the tracks, where it remained until it was replaced by a gambrel-roof masonry building in 1909. The branch between Bridgehampton and Sag Harbor was abandoned on May 3, 1939. *(Photo by G. B. Brainard; Brooklyn Public Library.)*

103

104

105

105. Whites only, Blacks only, Wainscott, ca. 1923. Whatever the laws of the State of New York may or may not have said on the subject, as late as the 1920s the L.I.R.R. maintained a bona fide Jim Crow railroad station at Wainscott, midway between Bridgehampton and East Hampton on the Montauk Branch. Few people utilized the facility in the long off-season, but during the summer months, the clientele consisted mainly of wealthy summer residents who owned fine houses in the area and Negro migrant farmers who worked the Sagaponack potato fields. Since the former did not wish to mingle with the latter in the cramped waiting room of a small rural depot, they requested—and were given—segregated facilities by the railroad. One of just two known photographs of the desolate structure, this picture clearly shows the two smoke jacks leading from pot-bellied stoves in the separate waiting rooms located to each side of the central agent's office. Wainscott was taken off the timetable during the Depression and the station building was converted into an ocean-front summer home. *(Photo by James V. Osborne; author's collection.)*

106. Early horseless carriages, Amagansett, September 19, 1911. Even in 1911, Amagansett was still a long way out on the South Fork of the East End of Long Island and it took a spirit of adventure to drive there on the Montauk Highway. Joseph Burt, the renowned Mineola photographer, made an all-day trip this day and exposed a goodly number of five-by-seven-inch dry plates between the Shinnecock Canal and Napeague Beach, including this one at the brand-new station. The original 1895 depot had burned the previous year, prompting the company to erect this impressive gambrel-roof structure to replace it. In June 1942, in

what was to be the only assault on the continental United States by armed Germans, a gang of saboteurs came ashore from a submarine and boarded a train for New York at this station. They were later caught and their plans of havoc were foiled. In 1964, when the administration of L.I.R.R. President Thomas M. Goodfellow announced plans to raze this fine building, a group of retired railroaders who lived nearby requested that the building be turned over to them to use as a railway museum and to continue to let passengers find shelter there. Incredibly, although Goodfellow was the most publicity-minded chief executive in the railroad's history, he rejected the idea and wantonly destroyed the structure, leaving an ugly and exposed little shed in its place. While the railroad was justified in tearing down some of the old stations, this vandalism of so fine a building was totally unwarranted and can only be described as an atrocity. *(Photo by J. Burt.)*

107. Napeague Beach, September 19, 1911. Overlooking the right-of-way of the railroad as it stretches eastward toward Montauk over the horizon, this view was from the bluffs east of Amagansett. The well-manicured single track, with a Montauk-bound train nearly a mile away, is the only sign of human encroachment, except for a pole line crossing the dunes to the south. Beyond the dunes to the right is the Atlantic Ocean; to the left is Napeague Harbor. A similar angle today reveals the paved Montauk Highway alongside the track and hundreds of houses connected by crisscrossing roads in the dunes. Only the railroad itself conveys even a modicum of timelessness in an area that has changed so radically in so short a time. *(Photo by J. Burt; author's collection.)*

108. Main entrance to concourse, Pennsylvania Station, 1910. The primary reason that the powerful and far-flung Pennsylvania Railroad purchased a controlling interest in the Long Island Rail Road was to gain direct access to mid-Manhattan, outflanking its mortal rival the New York Central, which had maintained its main terminal there for decades. The little L.I.R.R. possessed a franchise to enter Manhattan, but no capital, while the P.R.R. commanded virtually unlimited resources but no franchise. Once the Pennsy had bought the L.I.R.R., it wasted no time in using the franchise and its immense financial power to launch what was to be the largest and most expensive free-enterprise engineering project in history: the Pennsylvania Tunnel & Terminal Railroad. As the immense station took shape, few realized that it would become more of a commuting station than a terminal for posh long-distance limiteds. Even in its early history, more L.I.R.R. trains used Penn Station than did the owner itself. By 1960, over two-thirds of all trains rolling into its cavernous depths were Long Island electrics. Indeed, the first revenue train into the great "Temple of Transportation" (as an enthusiastic press had nicknamed it), was neither the great Pennsylvania Limited, nor the "Spirit of St. Louis," nor any other P.R.R. flagship; rather it was a humble train of L.I.R.R. MP-54 multiple-unit cars. The L.I.R.R. had begun daily service to Penn Station on September 8, 1910—two months before the first Pennsy varnish runs arrived! *(Library of Congress.)*

109. Midday activity at train gates, Penn Station, World War II Era. The construction of Penn Station was an immense undertaking that cost a staggering $125 million in 1910 (close to $10 billion today). Of course, the far greater part of the sum had been expended on tunneling beneath the Hudson River, through Manhattan Island and beneath the East River to Long Island City, where the Sunnyside Yard (the world's biggest passenger-car yard) received and dispatched every train from and to the mainland. But the tunnel work was largely hidden from the public view while the daily progress of the station building was witnessed by thousands of people over a five-year period. The figures for materials consumed in just the station facilities were impressive enough: covering almost eight acres, between Seventh and Eighth Avenues and 31st and 33rd Streets, it consisted of 27,000 tons of structural steel, more than 15,000,000 bricks and nearly 1,000,000 cubic feet of concrete, faced with 500,000 cubic feet of granite and topped with 220 tons of three-eighths-inch wire glass. When this early-1940s midday crowd is considered, it is not hard to imagine how well over one billion people could have used the station in the brief fifty-four years of its existence. The decline of the once-omnipotent Pennsylvania Railroad combined with an increasingly unbearable tax burden to force the Pennsy to demolish the grand station in the 1960s and replace it with the usual glass and chrome tombstones that have turned Manhattan into an architectural graveyard. Below ground level, much has remained unchanged—the tracks, platforms, signals and train movements—but the smog-filtered sun no longer shines on one of the great architectural treasures of history. *(Library of Congress.)*

108

110. New York World's Fair station, 1939. The winter of 1938–39 saw the United States emerging from the Great Depression, buoyed by renewed confidence, still three years away from entering the war that would begin in Europe just months later, so a big national celebration appeared in order. And celebrate we did, with the grand exposition in the Borough of Queens: the 1939–40 New York World's Fair. Although World War II began even before the Fair's first season closed, the Fair was a rousing success—in no small part due to the efforts of the Long Island Rail Road. Although taken a half-century ago, as the Fair was nearing completion early in 1939, this aerial photograph of the L.I.R.R. station (with one of the city's Transit Authority subway-car shops in the foreground) reveals a futuristic concept that would not be out of place on the most advanced high-speed rail line in France or Japan in the 1990s. The railroad was to haul millions of fairgoers with its "ten minutes for ten cents" ride from Penn Station, as well as long-distance excursion trains directly from the far reaches of the Pennsylvania Railroad and beyond, and this modern and efficient facility handled them all with dispatch. Unfortunately, after the two-season Fair closed, the L.I.R.R. had no further use for this depot, so it was demolished. *(Author's collection.)*

111. New elevated station, Rockville Centre, 1950. Painful memories of the head-on wreck in February 1950, in which thirty-five passengers were killed, were still heavy on the minds of the citizenry of Rockville Centre (or "Center," the form of the name depending on the fad of the moment) and the management of the railroad when the grade-crossing elimination was completed later that year. To make way for building the new embankment, a gantlet track, in which the two main tracks overlapped, had been utilized. It was on this section in Rockville Centre that the wreck had occurred. In this photo a solid train of the L.I.R.R.'s famous "double-deckers" (actually the cars had only one center deck; the passengers stepped up or down to their seats) is halted at the high station. Although the railroad had begun elevating the Montauk Branch in Nassau County in the 1930s, the vast project was not finished for forty years and has been continued into Suffolk County, its final form still in conjecture. Here, halfway through the twentieth century, Long Islanders glimpsed the twenty-first. *(Photo by Irving Solomon; author's collection.)*

CHAPTER SEVEN

Nautical Operations

112. Steamboat *Montauk* backing off Orient dock, ca. 1905. In the mid-nineteenth century, when the shorefront villages that had been bypassed by the Main Line of the Long Island Rail Road began clamoring for modern transportation, rival railroads and steamboat companies were quick to respond. By 1895, the Montauk Steam Boat (M.S.B.) Company had become a large operation whose trim white boats, sailing from the East River to Glenwood Landing, Greenport, Shelter Island, Sag Harbor and Montauk, as well as intermediate points, were giving the railroad stiff competition. In 1898, the L.I.R.R. bought out the M.S.B. Company and continued to run its vessels, coordinating the schedules with those of its trains. The M.S.B. Company purchased the three-year-old *Queen Caroline* in 1905, renamed her *Montauk* (the second vessel to carry that name) and set her to work on June 27 of that year. She was a fine, seaworthy little boat and alternated on the longer runs with the much larger *Shinnecock* through the teens, finally being sold to a New England line, where she was renamed *Transford*. *(Photo by Hal B. Fullerton; Suffolk County Historical Society.)*

113

113. S. S. *Sagamore*, Glenwood Landing, July 27, 1913. Many of the prominent stockbrokers, attorneys and other businessmen who commuted from Glen Cove, Sea Cliff and other points along the Oyster Bay Branch preferred the slower but more relaxed and refined ambiance provided by the steamboats to that of the wooden parlor cars of the railroad. Vessels such as the *Sagamore*, the *Nantasket* and the *Manhanset* were also convenient for them, sailing directly to James Slip in lower Manhattan, within walking distance of the counting houses of Wall Street. And, in case of severe weather or other problems, the steam cars of the L.I.R.R. always provided the more leisurely commuters with a reliable backup service. *(Photo by J. Burt; author's collection.)*

114. *Shinnecock* and other vessels, Long Wharf, Sag Harbor, ca. 1905. In this view looking down the slope to North West Harbor and the North Haven peninsula behind it, four children clad in white hike toward the road along the shore. The heavy summer steamboat traffic is evidenced by the flagship of the Montauk Steam Boat Company's fleet, the *Shinnecock*, and two smaller vessels tied up at Long Wharf. At the peak of its operations, the M.S.B. Company offered overnight service between Long Island City and Greenport, Shelter Island and Sag Harbor at a cost of two dollars for a stateroom, plus the regular fare. A varied menu was offered in the dining room and lounges, and a saloon provided ample room for passengers to relax. Today's generation can only marvel in envy at the thought of boarding the *Shinnecock* or the *Montauk* for a leisurely cruise the length of Long Island Sound, dining on fresh seafood, then walking the deck in the light of a rising full moon before retiring to a comfortable stateroom. At dawn, the boat called at Orient Point, then at the Manhanset House on Shelter Island, at Greenport, at the Prospect House and, an hour later, at Sag Harbor. Another vessel would make the reverse run in this popular summer service, offered from the 1890s to the 1920s. A regular schedule was also maintained from Sag Harbor and Montauk to Block Island. A vestige of the original intent of the Long Island Rail Road survived until 1927, in the form of the service from Greenport across the Sound, to New London, Connecticut. *(Author's collection.)*

115. The *Shinnecock* sails up the East River, ca. 1914. With the four-stacked Pennsylvania Railroad power plant on the Long Island City shore in the background, the pride of the Long Island Rail Road's fleet of white boats steams northward toward Long Island Sound. The slowly expanding influence of the Pennsy in L.I.R.R. affairs is evident in the form of a large keystone with the M.S.B. Company initials mounted on the funnel of the sleek coastal steamer. This view, probably taken from the deck of the *Sagamore*, shows the *Shinnecock* under full steam, the flag mounted over her stern blackened by the soft-coal smoke from her boilers, her amidships-located paddle wheel urging her forward at better than fifteen knots. Built in 1896, the *Shinnecock* was the prime asset of the Montauk Steam Boat Company when it was purchased by the L.I.R.R. just two years later. One of her first missions under her new owner in 1898 was to transport thousands of Spanish-American War veterans during their two-month quarantine at Camp Wyckoff on the barren dunes of Montauk. *(Photo by J. Burt; author's collection.)*

116

116. Photographer Burt on board the *Sagamore*, ca. 1914.
Joseph Burt was a dapper young man in his twenties when he
posed on board the *Sagamore*, probably at Glenwood Landing,
prior to one of his journeys on board the steamer to Long Island
City or James Slip in lower Manhattan. This four-by-five-inch
glass-plate photograph may have been taken by his wife Jenny,
herself an accomplished photographer. Although scattered
among several collections, most of Burt's important glass and
sheet-film negatives survive. *(Author's collection.)*

117. Steamboat *Wyandotte* sailing from Greenport, ca. 1920.
Built in 1892, the little *Wyandotte* retained her original name
after the L.I.R.R. purchased her in 1905. She served on all of the
M.S.B. Company routes, but she was sold in 1923 because of her
inability to handle the increasing automobile traffic. While the
Shinnecock was capable of carrying sixty cars, the *Wyandotte*
could squeeze no more than twenty onto her cramped deck. After
she left Long Island service the M.S.B. Company carried on for

just another four seasons, with the proud *Shinnecock* the flagship
to the end. *(Photo by Edith Young; author's collection.)*

118. Ferryboat *Sag Harbor*, East River ice floes, 1897. Once
the Long Island Rail Road opened its new terminal at Long Island
City in 1861, it began to provide ferry service directly to 34th
Street in Manhattan. When the Second and Third Avenue
elevated railroads were built in the 1870s, they provided a direct
spur line to the L.I.R.R. ferry terminal. By the 1890s, 35,000
commuters crossed the East River from this terminal each day.
The railroad owned a succession of double-ended ferries, mostly
a configuration similar to that of the *Sag Harbor*, which was built
in Newburgh, New York, in 1884. On all of these, the central open
section carried teams and wagons, while a spacious cabin ran the
outside length of the ferry on each side, one reserved for women
and the other for men. *(Photo by Hal B. Fullerton; Suffolk County
Historical Society.)*

119

120

119. Interior of ferry *Hempstead,* **1906.** The railroad operated seventeen different ferries across the East River, most of which were built between 1859 and 1884. Even though the tunnels to Manhattan were well on the way to completion, the L.I.R.R. ordered two final vessels in 1906, the *Hempstead* and the *Babylon.* Although the double-enders were short-run utilitarian craft, their interiors featured decor that, while not opulent, was certainly decorative, including fluted-column lampposts, smaller curlicued brass lights with flower shades, and spiral railings separating each seat from the next. The investment in the latter two boats was justified by the fact that, despite the opening of direct electric train service to Manhattan in 1910, the ferries survived in daily service for another fifteen years. *(Seth Bramson collection.)*

120. Ferryboat *Hempstead* **when new, 1906.** The background of this photo does not resemble anything on the East River, so this may well be a shakedown run at the time the vessel was built, in Wilmington, Delaware, in 1906. Larger and more modern than her predecessors, the *Hempstead* had two stacks and an iron hull with wooden superstructure. The keystones on the stacks are lettered "Long Island," since the ferries were owned directly by the railroad and not the subsidiary Montauk Steam Boat Company. Wheelhouses and bows at each end eliminated the need to turn before docking, greatly speeding up the operation of the ferries. *(Seth Bramson collection.)*

121. Launching of tugboat *Syosset,* **Philadelphia, April 29, 1899.** Beginning in the 1880s, freight cars were floated across New York Harbor between riverside railroad terminals in New Jersey and Long Island, ending the expensive and time-consuming process of transferring freight from railroad cars to barges and back to cars at the other end. All of the railroads involved soon acquired their own tugboats and carfloats. In 1899, the L.I.R.R. purchased its first steel-hulled tug, the *Syosset,* from Cramp's Shipyard in Philadelphia. A launching—be it of a battleship or a tug—is always a festive occasion, and several hundred Long Islanders rode a special train to Philadelphia as guests of the railroad. Here, L.I.R.R. officials, their wives and other interested parties, as well as yard workers, are seen milling about the boat and the pier shortly before the *Syosset* slid down the ways. *(Photo by Hal B. Fullerton; author's collection.)*

122

122. Ice-clogged East River and L.I.R.R. floats, February 3, 1945. During severe winters, such as that of 1944-45, heavy ice can clog not only the Hudson River, but the East River as well. This dramatic view, seen from the crane house (which raised and lowered the tracks leading to the carfloats), shows a mid-Manhattan skyline still dominated by the Empire State, Chrysler and Rockefeller Center buildings. In the foreground, a trio of L.I.R.R. tugs works in the broken ice, while floats loaded with freight cars wait to be unloaded by switch engines. More than half the cars are loaded with coal for the state hospitals, power plants, industry and the many homes that still used "Pennsylvania real estate" for fuel. Today, only the Kings Park State Hospital still burns coal, all the rest having switched to gas or oil since World War II. *(Author's collection.)*

123. Tug *Long Island* tied up at Long Island City, ca. 1955. In a quiet moment, one of the older tugs, the *Long Island*, rests between duties nudging carfloats over to New Jersey. In the background are the No. 1 and No. 2 float bridges where barges loaded with freight cars were secured prior to unloading and loading. More sophisticated than real float bridges, which ac-

tually rose and fell with the tides, these were raised and lowered by cranes, providing a more stable and secure joint between the tracks on the floats and the land. Abandoned since the 1970s, the Long Island City float facilities were phased out during a precipitous drop in freight traffic, as were the ones at Bay Ridge, Brooklyn. In recent years, all freight has come to Long Island via the Hell Gate Bridge, but the Bay Ridge facilities are being refurbished as the L.I.R.R. tries to regain the freight business that it let slip away so carelessly. *(Photo by Irving Solomon; author's collection.)*

124. Diesel and steam tugs at Long Island City, ca. 1955. By the 1950s all of the surviving Long Island tugs had been converted to diesel power, as was the *Meitowax*, shown leaving the dock. In the background, a New York Central tug—still steam powered—moves out with a float bound for the Jersey City rail yards. By 1964, the L.I.R.R. had sold its last tugs and barges, but other railroads still delivered cars to Long Island City for a few more years. The waste in abandoning all of the float facilities is evident as millions of dollars were spent in the 1980s to partially restore them. *(Photo by Irving Solomon; author's collection.)*

CHAPTER EIGHT

Modern Long Island Steam Trains

125

125. Latter-day nonstandard engine, Oyster Bay, June 19, 1938. The Pennsylvania Railroad called itself "the standard railroad of the world" and set rigid rules of uniformity for everything from dining-car china and paint formulae to locomotive specifications and outhouse dimensions. For nearly three decades at the start of the twentieth century, however, it allowed its subsidiary, the Long Island Rail Road, to carry on its operations with a large degree of autonomy, totally out of character with Pennsy's normally rigid procedures. Although the P.R.R. began supplying steam locomotives to the L.I.R.R. as early as 1903, they were not to dominate the roster until 1930. As late as 1924, the L.I.R.R. purchased new engines from outside builders, rather than from Pennsy's own Juniata Shops in Altoona, Pennsylvania. Among the later nonstandard steamers on the Long Island roster were six G-53sd 4–6–0 ten-wheelers delivered by the American Locomotive Company's Brooks Works, in Dunkirk, New York, in 1917. They were rather ordinary little dual-service (passenger and freight) engines, as no. 141, posed here after taking water at Oyster Bay, illustrates, but they performed well and were not retired until 1949—when diesels began arriving on the property *en masse* and steam had just six years to go on the Island. *(Photo by Edward L. May.)*

126. Cab interior of new locomotive, 1913. The immediate predecessors of the G-53sd class were the G-53sc's (which were only slightly different), built at ALCO's Schenectady Works in 1913. Generally, the builder would take one formal side-view photograph of one engine out of an order, but it often made pictures of details as well. Here is a rare glimpse of the inside of the cab of no. 138, taken when she was rolled out of the factory. Mounted on the boiler backhead (actually the rear of the firebox)

are the various levers, valves, knobs, handles and gauges with which the crew ran the locomotive. At the top are the steam and air-pressure gauges; the diagonal bar extending from the center to the right is the throttle. At the lower right are the two brake stands—the larger for the train brake system, the smaller for the engine brakes. Mostly hidden behind the brake controls is the large reverse lever. The hydrostatic lubricator, which controlled the flow of lubricating oil to the pistons, air compressor and other appliances, is at the upper right, above the throttle. The curving pipes on either side lead to the injectors, ingenious devices that mixed live steam with cold water from the tender, drawing the water into the boiler. Because the firebox is wider than most of that era, two fire doors were used, instead of the customary single centered door, allowing the fireman more flexibility in slinging coal. Later, larger locomotives reverted to a single set of doors. *(Alco Historic Photos.)*

127. Thundering through Mineola, July 1, 1955. Just four months before the end of steam operations, the last of the big grimy and sooty old iron horses still performed in the grand manner of old as they ran out their final miles before being sent to the scrap yards of Pennsylvania. Here H-10s 2–8–0-type freight engine no. 111, one of just three survivors of an original nineteen that were the heaviest freight power on the railroad for nearly three decades, shakes the ground at Nassau Tower in Mineola as she rolls by with a heavy train. Although their sixteen sisters had already been scrapped, nos. 108, 111 and 113 were utilized daily, until the very end of steam, for the specific task of handling the heaviest freight trains, since it would take two brand-new diesels to replace each of the forty-year-old steamers. *(Photo by Art Huneke.)*

128. Freight engine on turntable, Oyster Bay, ca. 1948.
Turning a locomotive could be accomplished in either of two
ways—and the L.I.R.R. made good use of both. One used a
triangular configuration of track with switches at the ends, called
a *wye*, in which the engine entered facing one way and emerged—
after three separate moves—facing in the opposite direction. A
more expensive setup, but one requiring much less space, was the
turntable. At various times, the railroad maintained turntables at
such locations as Long Island City, Locust Valley, Riverhead,
Jamaica, Whitestone Landing, Babylon, Patchogue, Morris Park,
Oyster Bay and Greenport. Although the latter three are still in
existence, just the Morris Park one is still serviceable. Wyes were
used at Montauk, Speonk, Wading River, Port Jefferson, Ronkonkoma, South Farmingdale and elsewhere. *(Photo by Robert B.
Morgan; author's collection.)*

129. Approaching Cold Spring Hill, May 1951. Westbound
from Huntington, Consolidation no. 106 pulls the local freight
from Port Jefferson at West Rogue's Path, about to descend Cold
Spring Hill, the longest heavy grade on the L.I.R.R. The diamond-
shaped crossing signs, once found all over the railroad, were gone
by the late 1960s, and this stretch of track was electrified as far as
Huntington in 1970. More recently, a second track was installed to
accommodate the rapidly growing population along the north
shore of western Suffolk County. *(Photo by John Krause; author's
collection.)*

130. Switching King's Park Hospital, early spring, 1951. For
many years, the railroad did a booming business serving the vast
state hospitals, built for the most part early in the twentieth
century. Each had its own central power plant and, until well
after the Second World War, they all burned coal. The L.I.R.R.
had brought in all of the materials used to construct the hospital
complexes, and later it carried the provisions necessary to sustain
them and their thousands of patients. On weekends, the L.I.R.R.
ran visitor trains and there even were special cars to transport the
insane, equipped with restraining seat belts and bars on the
windows. But the main commodity was coal. Here no. 107 is
backing several hopper cars down to the King's Park powerhouse,
whose twin stacks rise behind the trees at right. Today, this
facility remains the last regular coal customer on the Long Island
Rail Road, all others having changed to gas or oil. *(Photo by John
Krause; author's collection.)*

130

131

131. Switching King's Park Hospital, midwinter, ca. 1952.
Very few photographers of the railroad scene on Long Island ever
ventured onto the grounds of the hospitals. This was unfortunate,
for the photo opportunities were abundant indeed. Steaming
through the oak forest on snow-covered rails, this ex-
Pennsylvania Railroad engine—now owned by the L.I.R.R.—looks
for all the world as though she were working a branch line in the
Allegheny Mountains of her native Keystone State. Soon the
contents of the four coal hoppers behind her tender would be
making steam to power the hospital's generators and heat its
buildings. *(Photo by John Krause; author's collection.)*

**132. Engine no. 111 gives Stony Brook station a steam bath,
ca. 1951.** On a damp autumn day, condensing steam oozing from a
freight engine drifts lazily across the main track to virtually
envelop the little country depot. The conductor and the head
brakeman walk along the platform, while a third crewman stands

behind. The freight has taken the siding to allow a passenger train
to hold the main. Once the latter passes, the crew will receive
clearance to continue westbound, working the sidings that serve
the light industries and lumberyards along the Port Jefferson
Branch. *(Photo by John Krause; author's collection.)*

133. Crossing Mill Creek Bridge, Southold, ca. 1952. The
Greenport freight made the second-longest run on the railroad,
heading eastward from Holban Yard, Hollis, on Monday, Wed-
nesday and Friday and returning, after an overnight layover, on
Tuesday, Thursday and Saturday. Although the view of the rustic
little wooden trestle across Mill Creek, between Greenport and
Southold, as seen from the paralleling Main Road bridge, offered
fine photographic possibilities, this is the only known picture of a
steam train crossing the span. *(Photo by John Krause; author's
collection.)*

134. Grimy no. 108 at Southold station, 1952. The H-10s freight locomotives were dirty to begin with, but when they were equipped with automatic stokers, immediately following World War II, they became notorious air polluters. Although seen here with a clean stack as she is drifting to a stop while switching the lumberyard in Southold, no. 108 was really in her element chuffing along the Main Line, spewing a very photogenic cloud of soft-coal smoke, which drifted over homes and wash lines, irritating the railroad's neighbors. Since the retirement of steam, most households have been modernized with clothes dryers; but when the likes of no. 108 were spreading soot and cinders, the white sheets hung in the backyard in the morning were often gray by noon! *(Photo by John Krause; author's collection.)*

135. Assembling a train for the run to Holban, Riverhead, 1951. After working every potato-house and lumberyard siding between Greenport and Riverhead, the local freight engine would consolidate the train in the yard in the middle of Riverhead. Then it would run nonstop into Holban Yard, pausing only at Ronkonkoma to take on water. Here, no. 108, the locomotive regularly assigned to the Greenport freight during the last four years of steam, crosses Osborn Avenue as she switches the yard. As late as 1953, one of these relatively small engines would bring in as many as 110 carloads—over 5,000 tons—of potatoes during the autumn harvest season. Now, it all goes by truck—as any motorist battling traffic on the Long Island Expressway will ruefully testify. *(Photo by John Krause; author's collection.)*

136. Grooming a big goat, Morris Park, March 27, 1937. Steam locomotives designed specifically for yard switching were characterized by the absence of leading or trailing wheels, all of their weight being carried on the drivers. Limited by the very nature of their work to slow speeds, they had no need for the smaller wheels to guide them into curves. Also, with all of their weight on the driving wheels, they exerted more traction, enabling them to pull heavy loads. As the business of the L.I.R.R. increased rapidly in the teens and twenties, the railroad found that the older 0-6-0 "yard goats" could no longer handle the heavy switching chores. The solution was to go for the much larger 0-8-0 type, and, between 1916 and 1924, the L.I.R.R. ordered nineteen of the big brutes. Here, a maintenance man adjusts the lubricators on the siderods of no. 259 in the big engine terminal west of Jamaica. *(Photo by Hilliard N. Proctor; author's collection.)*

137. Switch engine on the Main Line, Mineola, May 22, 1948. Although their primary function was to switch yards and industrial sidings, shunters occasionally got out onto the high iron, as no. 253 did here. Even this early, the C-51sa class of eight-wheel switchers was nearing the end. With ninety-five percent of their work performed in Brooklyn and Queens (it is entirely possible that they never ran in Suffolk County), much of it in residential areas, they were the first steamers to be replaced with diesels. Thirteen of them were scrapped in 1949 alone, including no. 253, and only a trio of them was still around by 1951. *(Photo by John Krause; author's collection.)*

138. Ronkonkoma commuter train, March 6, 1949. Ever since the opening of the East River tunnels and Penn Station in Manhattan, the Long Island Rail Road's unfortunate destiny has been to convey commuters to and from their daily jobs. In 1910, the year that direct train service to midtown was inaugurated, just one-third of the L.I.R.R.'s business was the hauling of commuters; less than two decades later this ratio became two-thirds and has remained so ever since. (This is unfortunate because, with the vast number of employees and large amount of equipment necessary to maintain rush-hour service, commuter systems can never hope to recoup their high overhead through operating revenues.) So involved in commuter service has the L.I.R.R. been that, when the parent Pennsylvania Railroad designed what was to be the only locomotive ever built specifically for rapid-acceleration stop-and-start suburban main-line use, the Long Island immediately began ordering the engines for its own use. The result was the famous G-5s 4-6-0 "Pittsburgh Commuter Engine," which the P.R.R. initially assigned to pull heavy trains up into the hilly suburbs of the steel and commercial center. The Pennsy was to build ninety of the burly ten-wheelers for its own use, and the L.I.R.R. ordered thirty-one additional engines for itself between 1924 and 1929—the last new steamers to be built for the L.I.R.R. Here, the first Long Island G-5s—no. 20—makes short work of a seven-car local at Ronkonkoma. *(Photo by John Krause; author's collection.)*

139. Taking water at Ronkonkoma, October 23, 1949. At 118 tons in operating order, the G-5s was the heaviest and largest ten-wheeler ever to go into production. With its sixty-eight-inch driving wheels, the bulky 4-6-0 was easily capable of accelerating to seventy miles per hour and was known to nudge eighty when making up lost time. Its most desirable characteristic in commuter service, however, was its ability to effect jackrabbit starts and then to stop very quickly when running between suburban stations that were located just two to five miles apart. One of the duties of the fireman was to fill the water tank of the tender, as he is doing here, behind engine no. 37. *(Photo by John Krause; author's collection.)*

140. Engine no. 32 at Glen Cove, 1949. Accelerating away from the Glen Street depot, a G-5s illustrates the capabilities of the species. While they were good steamers and could even handle seventy-car freights, they were very rough-riding and crewmen who worked them steadily for years actually could develop intestinal problems. Lacking a trailing truck beneath the cab, and with an inordinately long space between the second and third sets of driving wheels, the G-5s was prone to gyrating and bouncing at speeds over fifty miles per hour. Still, it was a sound design of typical Pennsylvania rugged simplicity that performed its intended tasks with competence and, in its basic way, an air of crude dignity. *(Photo by John Krause; author's collection.)*

141. End of the line for engine no. 29, Huntington station, 1950. On the afternoon of August 6, 1950, as G-5s no. 29 with a passenger train in tow was racing toward Huntington, a rookie brakeman on the local freight, which was on a siding, misunderstood a hand signal from the freight's conductor and opened the switch. Before he could hear the frantic conductor rushing toward him and shouting, the passenger train roared into the siding and clobbered the standing freight. Fortunately, several empty cars—including a wooden boxcar—were coupled ahead of the freight engine, absorbing the shock. Since the railroad was buying many new diesels at the time, both of the wrecked steamers were scrapped immediately after the mishap. The crew of no. 29 and seventy-five passengers were injured in this, the last L.I.R.R. wreck involving two steam locomotives. *(Photo by F. J. Weber; author's collection.)*

142. Crossing Bread and Cheese Hollow trestle, King's Park, March 19, 1950. The long high trestle over Bread and Cheese Hollow Road, which forms the boundary between the Towns of Huntington and Smithtown, was a favorite location for railway photographers in the last years of steam. The location got the odd but colorful name when colonist Richard Smith, for whom Smithtown was named, was promised by the Indians all of the land that he could traverse while riding a bull betwen sunrise and sunset. For nourishment he carried bread and cheese, which he ate while riding through the hollow now spanned by the Port Jefferson Branch of the L.I.R.R. The local Indians honored their pledge and gave Smith the land that, more than three centuries later, still bears his name. *(Photo by John Krause; author's collection.)*

143. Commuter trains laid up at Port Jefferson, April 24, 1938. The high cost of providing rush-hour commuter service is illustrated by these three trains waiting their next calls to duty. The fact is that in a commuting situation, seventy percent of the locomotives, cars and crews are needed just thirty percent of the time, that is, eight hours a day, five or six days a week. The remaining idle time results in very low utilization of equipment and manpower—and high expenses. As built, the G-5s engines had round number plates (seen in this photo), but, in 1942, the Pennsy ordered that the keystone-shaped plates that were standard for its own passenger locomotives also be installed on the Long Island's G-5s power. The G-5s locomotive wrote the final chapter in the L.I.R.R. steam story, after 120 years, when they pulled the last steam trains, in October 1955. The last four to run were nos. 35, 38, 39 and 50. Ultimately, 35 and 39 were preserved—the only Long Island-owned steamers to escape the torch. Three of the Pennsylvania locomotives now preserved in the State Railroad Museum at Strasburg also were leased to the L.I.R.R. for short periods of time. *(Photo by George E. Votava.)*

141

144

144. Wintry departure, Port Jefferson, 1954. Steam locomotives were always more photogenic on cold winter days, when the exhaust steam would condense into vast fleecy plumes of white. If the engine was smoking as well, black and gray would mingle with the steam, creating the most beautiful pollution imaginable! Here, no. 50, the highest-numbered G-5s and the newest steam locomotive purchased by the L.I.R.R. (she had been delivered in January 1930), blasts upgrade out of the Port Jefferson yard, bound for Jamaica. *(Photo by John Krause; author's collection.)*

145. Steam and "ping-pong" coaches, Mineola, 1948. The steel coach design chosen to replace the wooden cars early in the century became the predominant type of passenger carrier on the L.I.R.R. for sixty years—surviving for nearly two decades after the last steamers were retired. Based on the design of the MP-54 electric cars of 1908, the design of the steam-train cars was virtually identical; in fact, quite a few were converted to electric service after the electrification to Babylon in 1925. As requirements changed, some electric cars were even converted to steam service! Because of their light weight, these cars tended to give a bouncy ride, especially when coupled between the locomotive and

heavier cars behind, leading L.I.R.R. trainmen to nickname them "ping-pongs," or simply "pings." The last were retired in 1974, along with the old electrics, ending the last vestige of Pennsylvania Railroad influence on Long Island. *(Photo by John Krause; author's collection.)*

146. "Fish Train" at Montauk, ca. 1940. For many years, the railroad ran the "Fisherman's Special" to Montauk, with a stop at the Shinnecock Canal. Hundreds of anglers would board the train at Jamaica before dawn, and, with no stops at an early hour when traffic was light, the special—pulled by eighty-inch-driving-wheeled Pennsylvania Railroad steam engines—would attain legendary speeds as it raced to the party-boat docks at Hampton Bays and Montauk. Returning in the evening, the fishermen would tag their catches and deposit them in ice bunkers in the baggage car, claiming them at the end of the run. Despite the convenience and popularity of these trains, the fishermen long ago forsook the practicality of the "Fish Train" to make the grueling drive to Montauk in their own automobiles, causing the railroad to reluctantly terminate the service in the 1960s. *(Author's collection.)*

CHAPTER NINE

People and the
Long Island Rail Road

147.

147. Officials at Riverhead Fair, 1908. Long Island Rail Road President Ralph Peters, wearing gloves despite the September weather, along with other railroad officials, hosted the Hon. Edward Thompson at the railroad's demonstration-farm pavilion at the annual Suffolk County Fair at Riverhead. This was the time when the L.I.R.R. was the largest employer and the most important and influential business enterprise on Long Island, so the president often attended civic functions to burnish the image and further the goals of the company. When President William H. Baldwin died in January 1905, he was succeeded by his able superintendent, William F. Potter, who promptly contracted spinal meningitis and died just three months after Baldwin. The parent Pennsylvania Railroad then sent Peters to Long Island and he ran the company for eighteen years, retiring at the mandatory age of seventy, in 1923. Peters, having taken charge just as the first stage of electrification was nearing completion, led the railroad through the most spectacular period of growth in its history. An amiable man, Peters was well respected by all whom he dealt with, including the rank-and-file railway men who worked so hard to keep the company running smoothly. *(Photo by Hal B. Fullerton; Suffolk County Historical Society.)*
148. Railroad police officers, Jamaica station, ca. 1920. As early as the 1840s, the L.I.R.R. hired armed guards to ride trains and patrol the tracks in Suffolk County to protect railroad property against violence perpetrated by angry residents of the

East End who, more likely than not, were prone to settling disputes against the company by derailing trains and burning stations. And disputes there were—involving everything from "Sabbath-breaking" (running trains on Sunday) to the railroad's refusing to reimburse farmers when locomotives killed livestock or set fields of grain afire. An act of the state legislature empowered railways to maintain their own police forces, and, by World War I, the L.I.R.R. had a sizable uniformed force. This group includes the captain, three lieutenants, seven sergeants and eighteen men—probably not the entire force at the time. (It is uncertain who the additional man not in uniform was.) In recent times, railroad police have been made peace officers with full police powers and the force has numbered almost 200 men. *(Photo by F. J. Weber; The Queens Borough Public Library.)*
149. Towerman, "PD" tower, Patchogue, ca. 1925. This unidentified leverman, dapper in his celluloid collar, tie and vest, dressed much more formally than his successors do today. The big levers in front of him controlled the switches in the Patchogue yard. He also worked the crossing gates across South Ocean Avenue, as well as the semaphore signals that governed train movements. The L.I.R.R. still maintains a number of towers (including this one) whose function is to control train movements, much as air-traffic controllers govern the movements of jet airliners today. *(Photo by James V. Osborne; author's collection.)*

150. A proud engineer and his monogrammed locomotive, June 1924. In the earliest years of railroading, specific locomotives were assigned to senior engineers, who lavished great attention on the machines—decoratively, as well as mechanically. In 1924, amid much favorable publicity, including an editorial in *The New York Times*, the L.I.R.R. revived the custom and lettered the names of its half-dozen most senior engineers on the cabs of their regular engines. Appropriately, Speonk native Edward W. Hulse, who, in his mid-fifties, was the ranking engineman, was assigned camelback 4–4–2 no. 1. This locomotive carried his name for eighteen months, and, when he was assigned a brand-new G-5s locomotive, no. 27, his name adorned that one. The legendary experiences of "hoggers" (steam engines were called "hogs," so engineers were dubbed "hoggers") such as Hulse found their way into the local folklore of Long Island—along with the Indians, the whalers, the Spanish-American War and the 1938 hurricane. *(Author's collection.)*

151. The Trainmen's Trio, Jamaica, ca. 1925. During the 1920s, culture rode the rails of the Long Island Rail Road. This included a large company band, the Ralph Peters Singing and Dramatic Society, an intramural sports program, which took Long Island athletes all over the region served by the Pennsylvania Railroad, and numerous other undertakings. One of the most popular groups was the Trainmen's Trio, a banjo-, guitar- and saxophone-playing, singing combo that appeared at countless public events, leaving a wide swath of good will for the railroad in their wake. Founded in 1924 by (from left to right in the photo) trainmen Jefferson Skinner, John Diehl and Matthew Balling, the Trio played on for more than twenty years, with Charles H. Burton replacing Diehl later on. With the onset of the Great Depression and the national malaise it spawned, all of the fine athletic and artistic programs of the railroad were disbanded—except for the Trainmen's Trio, which survived until the railroad finally abdicated its leadership role in the affairs of Long Island. Jeff Skinner outlived his compatriots, retiring in the late 1960s after a half-century of working on the railroad he loved. *(Author's collection.)*

151

150

152

152. Sunrise Trail Band, railroad dock, Greenport, ca. 1925.
During the 1920s one of the first large-scale public media
campaigns was waged on a long-term basis to lure visitors and
new residents to Long Island. A combined effort of business and
civic groups and newspapers, the "Hit the Sunrise Trail" promotion was led by the railroad. Named for the famed Indian trail
along the island's south side, the effort sparked greatly increased
tourism—by road and rail—as well as large-scale residential and
commercial development. The railroad even named its premier
train the Sunrise Special (the name still used on one of the
weekend trains to the Hamptons), and its athletic teams were
called the Sunrise Trails. The renowned L.I.R.R. Sunrise Trail
Band played at many public functions, rode the trains, enter-
tained on the steamboats and—to judge by contemporary news-
paper accounts—played very well, earning numerous awards and
accolades. Ironically, one lasting legacy of the 1920s' promotion,
the Sunrise Highway, leading from the Queens County line to
Southampton, would siphon off much of the passenger and freight
business of the railroad. The Sunrise Trail Band, like so many of
the fine morale-boosting efforts of the L.I.R.R., was discontinued
in 1931 as the depression deepened. *(Author's collection.)*

153. The engineer of the Cannon Ball in his "office," July 1937.
When the L.I.R.R. was extended to Montauk in 1895, the engine
terminal was established at Amagansett, a full fifteen miles west
of the end of track, since few trains ran all the way initially. The
purpose that had prompted President Austin Corbin to build the
Montauk extension from Bridgehampton was his vision of a deepwater port at Fort Pond Bay, which at the time was inhabited only
by shepherds and a few hearty summer adventurers. Since
Amagansett was the easternmost village, regular trains terminated there until Montauk was finally developed in the 1920s.
Quite a few railroad families lived in Amagansett, the most
famous being the Eichhorns, several generations of whom became
engineers and conductors. By 1937, James C. Eichhorn, Sr., was
number one on the seniority roster, and he regularly ran the crack
Cannon Ball to Montauk, often at the throttle of what was perhaps
the most popular steam locomotive on the roster, leased Pennsy
K-4s Pacific no. 5406. Just six months after this photo was taken in
the cab of the 5406, Eichhorn retired. A poster was printed to
promote a testimonial dinner attended by over sixty prominent
men, featuring this picture and the slogan "We've all ridden
behind 'Old Jim'—now let's come out and dine with him."
(Author's collection.)

153

154. Attendants and conductors at Montauk, 1939. Extra-fare parlor cars have long been the hallmark of service that has set the Long Island Rail Road in a class apart from most other lines, including some many times more renowned and wealthy. Since its earliest days, the L.I.R.R. has regularly conveyed to the fashionable pristine ocean and bay beaches of the Island holidaying New York social aristocrats willing to pay for amenities not usually affordable by commuters or day-trippers. In the 1880s, the company ran a fleet of posh Woodruff parlor cars; by 1902, the number of parlor and similar club cars totaled forty-six—all owned by the railroad, and all of wood construction. The newest ones, built in 1902, rode on six-wheel trucks and had closed vestibules. These, the last of the wooden cars, weighed more than fifty-three tons—fourteen tons more than the later standard P-54 steel coaches! In those times, a parlor car was standard equipment on many long-distance trains; more recently, they have been used almost exclusively on summer weekend trains to the Hamptons, with one to Greenport. In a few instances, affluent commuter groups have leased them on a daily basis. With the completion of the changeover to a one-hundred-percent steel fleet by 1927, the L.I.R.R. had retired all of its wooden parlor cars and began leasing an array of club, buffet and lounge cars—even an open-end observation car—from the Pullman Company. In addition to providing individual plush revolving chairs, each of these cars had an attendant who served drinks and snacks to patrons in their seats. The dark-jacketed Black men in this picture were parlor car attendants. The white-coated man was probably a porter, perhaps on the through Pullman sleeper that once operated between Pittsburgh and Montauk on one of the weekend summer trains: *(The Queens Borough Public Library.)*

155

155. Serving patrons in a parlor car, late 1950s.
Because of the Depression and World War II, the L.I.R.R.
parlor-car service fell into disfavor; by the 1950s, just a
few cars remained. Then, publicity- and revenue-con-
scious Thomas M. Goodfellow—the Pennsylvania Railroad
official who then headed the L.I.R.R.—was given the task
of resuscitating the line in the aftermath of the fatal
wrecks of 1950. Goodfellow began leasing surplus P.R.R.
parlor cars in the late 1950s, then brought Walter F.
McNamara over as Manager of Special Services to completely revitalize the service. "Mac" soon purchased the
Pennsy cars, ultimately acquiring more than thirty 1920s-
era six-wheel-truck cars. The scruffy old Cannon Ball once
again became one of the finest trains in America and the
last all-parlor one as well, often running seventeen cars,
with an open-end observation car bringing up the rear.
The service flourished through the 1960s, but, with the
State of New York's taking over the L.I.R.R., Goodfellow's
departure to become President of the Association of
American Railroads, and the death of McNamara, the
magnificent old cars went to scrap. Today, the railroad's
parlor fleet is half the size it was in Goodfellow's time, and
the cars used are converted 1950s coaches, with loose,
movable furniture—an incredible setup that could cause
severe injuries even during a relatively low-speed derailment. *(Photo by Irving Solomon.)*

156. "Rosie the Riveter" on the L.I.R.R., 1942. War is
always the most trying time for railways, even those far
from the battle fronts. The L.I.R.R. was every bit as deeply
involved in World War II as it had been in the Spanish-
American War and First World War earlier. Camp
Upton, near Yaphank, was reactivated in 1940, and vital
war industries—most notably Republic Aviation, builder
of the P-47 "Thunderbolt," and Grumman, whose F4F
"Wildcat," F6F "Hellcat" and TBF "Avenger" were to
prove decisive in the Pacific war—were to claim much of
the resources of the railroad. In addition, severe gasoline
and tire rationing forced thousands of riders off the
highways and onto trains. Compounding the urgency was
the fact that nearly twenty percent of the company's work
force had gone into military service by 1943, many as
Army railroaders who served in sixteen countries. As
women took over formerly all-male jobs in industry, so did
they in transportation as well, and they acquitted themselves with competence and dignity on the L.I.R.R. Here,
five of the distaff engine maintainers at Morris Park give a
final wipe-down to G-5s no. 49, prior to the engine's being
turned over to her crew for the evening rush-hour commuter haulage. *(Author's collection.)*

157. A "Wheel" takes over a man's job, April 1943.
Wearing a feminine version of the standard Pennsylvania
Railroad trainman's uniform, scores of women went into
train service during World War II, working as brakemen,
ticket takers and inspectors. Nicknamed "Wheels" by
railroad men, they quickly took to the work, and their
male counterparts, as well as seasoned commuters, spoke
highly of their aplomb and competence. Here, a female
trainman consults her employee timetable to advise a
passenger on scheduling, while an Army sergeant looks on
with approval—perhaps even a touch of admiration. After
the war, the all-male policies were quickly reinstated, but
a quarter-century later, when women tried to break down
the old sexual barrier, they met with stiff resistance from
management, who claimed that women could not handle
the work. Having thus foolishly displayed their usual total
ignorance of the history of the company they are supposed
to be leading, the L.I.R.R. managers suffered an igno-
minious courtroom defeat when the union involved produced a photo of "Wheels" at work that had been published
in a previous work by the author of this book! *(Author's
collection.)*

158. Engine crew at work, Fresh Pond, ca. 1944. Short not only of manpower, but motive power as well during the Second World War, the Long Island Rail Road turned to parent Pennsy to lease ten of its medium-size L-1s 2-8-2 freight engines—the heaviest locomotives ever operated by the railroad. These engines often took over Bay Ridge–bound freights that had been brought over the Hell Gate Bridge by the New York, New Haven & Hartford Railroad, as no. 3590 was doing at Fresh Pond Junction when this photo was taken by a teenage boy who was to work on the L.I.R.R. as a brakeman a few years later. The freight version of the famed K-4s passenger engines (they had the same boiler and other subassemblies) that had been running on Long Island since 1931, the L-1s Mikados also were used to pull heavy potato extras westbound from Riverhead. Unfortunately, the combination of wartime photographic restrictions with the fact that most photographers of the L.I.R.R. scene were in the armed forces left precious few photos of the brief time (1944–46) that the L-1s spent on Long Island. *(Photo by Robert B. Morgan; author's collection.)*

159. "Princey" and his locomotive, ca. 1948. Long Island Rail Road old-timers recall many legendary characters from the steam era. One of the last generation was Clifford Prince ("Princey" to his fellow railroaders) who began his career in the teens and retired after more than forty years in engine service. Among his tales of days long gone was that of the time that he felt his big K-4s lurch at speed as he was racing through a blizzard after leaving East Hampton. Since a glob of gore had hit his arm, Princey assumed that he had killed a cow. When he arrived at Amagansett, he found the entire engine "covered with assorted cow parts, from the neck back." When he phoned a trackman later, he learned that the snow drifts along the track were littered with "six cows dead and one dyin'." The cowcatcher of his big 4-6-2 had done its job. *(Photo by Robert B. Morgan; author's collection.)*

160. Engineer and conductor comparing watches, Jamaica, 1955. The conductor, traditionally in charge of the train, would always set his pocket watch by a Standard Regulator clock whose accuracy would be closely monitored by the railroad. In turn, the other crew members would set their watches to conform with the conductor's timepiece. In this photo, taken just months before the L.I.R.R.'s final steam run in 1955, a uniformed old conductor with many years' service and his denim-clad engineer compare their watches in that most time-honored of all railroad rituals, prior to departing from Jamaica station. *(Author's collection.)*

161. Engineer of no. 39 works the brake, Morris Park, 1955. In a rare view of an L.I.R.R. engineer seated in the cab and running his locomotive, H. P. Voizard moves one of the last ten active steamers from the engine terminal to pick up his train. G-5s no. 39 was later chosen—along with identical sister no. 35—to be preserved for display to the public. After being the largest-sized relic in The Museums at Stony Brook from 1956 to 1980, no. 39 was moved to the railroad yard in Riverhead, where it has been undergoing a complete mechanical restoration with plans to run it in excursion service eventually. Although the Metropolitan Transportation Authority, the state agency that now runs the L.I.R.R., spends $300,000 annually to subsidize the subway museum in Brooklyn, it steadfastly refuses to grant any concessions to L.I.R.R. historical preservation, which is the reason that, after a decade of hard work, no. 39 is still not in running condition. *(Author's collection.)*

159

160

161

CHAPTER TEN

Yards and Maintenance Equipment

162. Looking east from Union Hall Street bridge, Jamaica, September 1897. The Main Line, just a few hundred feet east of Jamaica station, was still only two tracks wide until 1903, when extensive upgrading was done in anticipation of the imminent electrification. Once the line was clear of the bridges that carried Beaver Street, Washington Street and Union Hall Street over the railroad, switches led to paralleling freight tracks, which served the many commercial enterprises along the line. Despite the great increase in train traffic, the grade crossings in this photo were not eliminated for another thirty years. The "notice" sign in the left foreground admonished trespassers that "walking on the track is strictly forbidden." *(The Queens Borough Public Library.)*

163. Main freight yard, Jamaica, March 8, 1904. It is difficult to comprehend that this scene is the location of the present-day Jamaica station. Since the L.I.R.R. already owned this considerable property, it was a logical location for the vast new terminal, in the earliest planning stages at the time. Nine years after this photo was made, the station opened. In the intervening short time, the world's first main-line electrification was inaugurated (including the tracks at the near left), and hundreds of trainloads of fill were brought in from Cold Spring Hill on the Wading River Branch to raise the tracks up high above ground level. The Long Island's Engineering Department had planned with great foresight, for the 1913 station remains essentially the same as built and still handles the traffic efficiently. The freight yard was moved to Hollis (the Holban Yard), three miles eastward. The freight facilities, however, were displaced at Hollis by new shop facilities in the 1980s. *(Author's collection.)*

164. Gas plant and gas transport car, Jamaica, ca. 1904. The old wooden passenger cars were illuminated by Pintsch gas lamps, and each car mounted a tank to hold the gas. The outlying terminals had storage tanks, which were filled by periodic visits from the gas transport car, shown here at the plant, just east of Jamaica station, where the gas was manufactured. A new high-tension steel pole has already been erected and wired to carry the power lines for the initial electrification, which was to be placed in service in 1905. *(Photo by Hal B. Fullerton; author's collection.)*

165. Kaleidoscope of equipment, Morris Park, December 29, 1908. The first decade of the twentieth century saw the Long Island Rail Road evolve from its bucolic rural beginnings into a modern commuter line and, to a lesser extent, a long-distance and freight hauler. Nothing could illustrate better the metamorphosis being experienced by the company than this photo, showing the tracks that held equipment waiting to be worked on in the shop buildings behind. The old and the new mingled very freely, and a study of these cars and locomotives shows how the passenger roster was undergoing transition in 1908. At the extreme left in the photo is a narrow rapid-transit center-door coach used for running over the elevated railway connection and to the Brooklyn Bridge. Immediately adjacent is an MP-41 coach from 1905 (the MP-41's were the first electric cars and the world's first all-steel passenger cars). To left of center are two wooden coaches from the 1880s. At the center is a brand-new steel MP-54 electric car awaiting installation of headlights, markers, etc., prior to being placed in service. Cars of this type were built in the 1908–30 period, and some survived in regular service into the early 1970s. To right of center stands a closed-vestibule parlor car, built in 1902 as part of the last order of wooden steam passenger cars. Next to the shed is an 1870-era wooden baggage car. In front of the shed is the last of the "rapid-transit" tank engines, displaced by the 1905 electrification, but still used on Sag Harbor shuttle trains. Finally, at the extreme right is an 1899 E-1 camelback 4-4-2, no. 199, with a scale-test car in front. Since the railroad had to weigh cars loaded with coal, sand, potatoes and other bulk commodities, it maintained a number of heavy-duty scales. Weight-test cars were used to set the scales to ensure accuracy. *(Author's collection.)*

163

166

166. Engine-servicing facilities, Morris Park, September 6, 1931. Between runs, locomotives were inspected and serviced at Morris Park, the largest engine terminal on the L.I.R.R. The gantry in the foreground carried a large water main to the spouts, which filled tenders at the rate of a thousand gallons a minute. To the right is the coal tipple, from which as much as fourteen tons at a time could be loaded into a tender. The far gantry was a "stack scrubber," an early form of pollution control. Engines in the terminal were spotted so that the hoods on the structures could be lowered over their stacks. Live steam was sent through the pipe above, and, at the far end, a sludge of water and coal soot streamed out. Maintenance men found the device annoying to operate, and it was difficult to pinpoint the positions of locomotives to utilize the thing, so it was usually ignored, resulting in the blackening of houses, washlines and the reputation of the railroad in nearby Richmond Hill. *(Photo by F. J. Weber; author's collection.)*

167. Engine ready-tracks, Morris Park, 1948. The four locomotives facing the camera in the center of the picture have just returned from runs out east. The three passenger engines have left their trains at Jamaica station or the storage yard, the freight engine uncoupled at Holban Yard. They will proceed to the turntable and be either sent into the roundhouse for minor repairs, or turned and dispatched to the coal tipple and watering columns. Then they will join the cluster of locomotives at the right,

all awaiting their next calls to duty. *(Photo by Robert B. Morgan; author's collection.)*

168. Bay Ridge Yard, Brooklyn, August 21, 1931. In addition to the elaborate float-bridge facilities at Long Island City, the L.I.R.R. had a large yard to load and unload carfloats in Bay Ridge. This view, looking toward the waterfront, shows the four float gantries in the background. At this yard, freight cars from Long Island, as well as those delivered by the New Haven Railroad from New England, were classified and loaded on the floats for transfer to a half-dozen railroads on the New Jersey shore. The L.I.R.R. bought fourteen little six-wheel B-3 electric switch engines from the Pennsy in 1926, just to work the Bay Ridge Branch. Unlike the rest of the Long Island's electric lines, which were powered by third rail, this section was fed by overhead catenary, enabling New Haven electrics that had come over the Hell Gate Bridge to run right through and deliver their long trains to the little B-3s that shunted the floats. When the Pennsylvania Railroad sold the L.I.R.R. to the state, it retained the Bay Ridge Branch, then later abandoned it, scrapping all the facilities. More recently, the Long Island bought it back and—in conjunction with the City of New York—is spending many millions of tax dollars to restore the facilities, which should never have been destroyed in the first place! *(Photo by F. J. Weber; author's collection.)*

171

172

173

169. The oil train, Central Islip, July 6, 1899. In the days of steam, and before air-conditioning, dust and soot blowing into passenger cars caused a serious problem, coating the white bonnets and celluloid collars of hapless travelers in a variety of gray and brown tones. Fine cinder screens placed over window openings only partially alleviated the situation, so the L.I.R.R. each season sent out its oil train to spread its black goo along the right-of-way. In addition to holding down the dust, the oil also impregnated the ties, extending their service time; retarded the growth of vegetation; deterred trespassers; and aided drainage. *(Photo by Hal B. Fullerton; Suffolk County Historical Society.)*

170. "Caterpillar warfare," Montauk, 1913. In addition to being a residential and tourist paradise, Long Island was once an insect Valhalla as well. An early-spring infestation of caterpillars along the Montauk Branch in 1913 was so severe that locomotive wheels actually slipped as they ran over hordes of the insects, slowing and even stalling trains. A handcar and trailer loaded with barrels of chemicals and stirrup pumps was sent out, and an eleven-man crew doused the tracks, presumably winning a skirmish referred to by photographer Fullerton on the original glass-plate envelopes as "caterpillar warfare." *(Photo by Hal B. Fullerton; Suffolk County Historical Society.)*

171. Gasoline-powered inspection car, Jamaica, August 1905. The L.I.R.R. was modernizing in several ways in 1905. At the very time that the first electrified trackage went into service, the Maintenance of Way Department purchased what may well have been the first piece of internal-combustion equipment to be owned by the railroad. As basic as could be, the car lacked a transmission; its cylinder attached directly to the wheel by means of a driving rod—exactly the system used in propelling steam locomotives. *(Photo by Hal B. Fullerton; author's collection.)*

172. Gasoline section car, Woodhaven Junction, September 1, 1907. Just two years after the first diminutive gas car rode L.I.R.R. rails, a much larger version was in service, one that no doubt was capable of hauling trailers of tools and parts as well. These men, although well dressed by today's standards, were probably track workers. They are on the Rockaway Beach Branch; the Atlantic Branch (originally the Brooklyn & Jamaica Railroad) is in the background. *(Photo by Hal B. Fullerton; Suffolk County Historical Society.)*

173. Road-and-rail truck, Mastic, ca. 1948. The most important development in gasoline-powered vehicles for railroad use was that of the bimodal concept for maintenance and inspection trucks, resulting in trucks that could operate equally well on the highway or the rails. With retractable steel-flanged wheels mounted on an ordinary truck such as this one, assigned to the Patchogue section gang, work crews enjoyed much greater speed, flexibility and mobility than they knew with either a purely rail or purely road vehicle. Here, at the east end of the original Mastic station, the truck maneuvers on the Mastic Road crossing, preparatory to lowering the rail wheels and using the rear tires for power, as in road driving, and heading off down the track. Today, the railroad uses much larger trucks, enabling it to do work along the tracks that once required more expensive locomotives and rail cars to accomplish. *(Photo by Ed Minden; author's collection.)*

Yards and Maintenance Equipment 119

CHAPTER ELEVEN

Electric Operations

174. Testing an early electric locomotive, Garden City, 1908. Once the construction of the Pennsylvania Station and tunnels to Manhattan was undertaken, a technological race was begun to develop a reliable electric locomotive to propel trains to the terminal. Steam locomotives and wooden cars were expressly forbidden by law from using the facilities because engine exhaust would be deadly in the confined tunnels and the possibility of fire rendered wooden rolling stock far too risky. Pennsy engineers were working against a deadline of 1910, the opening date of the vast project, and they had to have a practical electric locomotive in production by then. Several designs were tested and some of the tests were conducted on a stretch of electrified track near Garden City. Locomotive no. 10003 proved the most successful design, and from it was developed the famed DD-1 fleet, which went into production beginning in 1909. When Penn Station opened, the electric locomotives were in service, taking over long trains of steel cars from steam engines at Manhattan Transfer, in New Jersey, and speeding them through the tunnels. Even today, the modern electric trains that speed along the Northeast Corridor can trace their beginnings back to the tests on Long Island in 1908. *(Collection of Edward T. Francis.)*

175. Pennsy's first electric engine on the L.I.R.R., September 4, 1932. The first P.R.R. electric locomotive, no. 10001, was built in 1905. It ultimately lost out to the 10003 in the testing phase, but it was kept working around Penn Station and Sunnyside Yard until 1916, when the Pennsy sold it to the Long Island. In L.I.R.R. service, it was used for switching and local freight service. Numbered 323 and known affectionately as "Phoebe" to railroaders, it was retired in 1937. Regrettably this pioneer locomotive, so important in railway history, was cut up for scrap. *(Photo by Harold Fagerberg.)*

176. MP-41 electric cars, Mineola, 1944. For the initial electrification of 1905, the L.I.R.R. ordered what were to be the world's first all-steel passenger cars built for main-line service. Since the original plans called for Long Island trains to run onto the subway tracks of the Interborough Rapid Transit line at Flatbush Avenue, Brooklyn, these 134 MP-41 cars were built for narrow clearances; in fact they were adapted by renowned engineer George Gibbs from his 1904 subway-car design. The scheme to run L.I.R.R. trains directly to Manhattan via the I.R.T. lines never materialized, so the small MP-41s were to spend most of their service lives as rapid-transit cars along the Atlantic Branch, on racetrack trains and the shuttle run to Mitchel Field, and in other uses as well. *(Photo by R. W. Wallendorf.)*

174

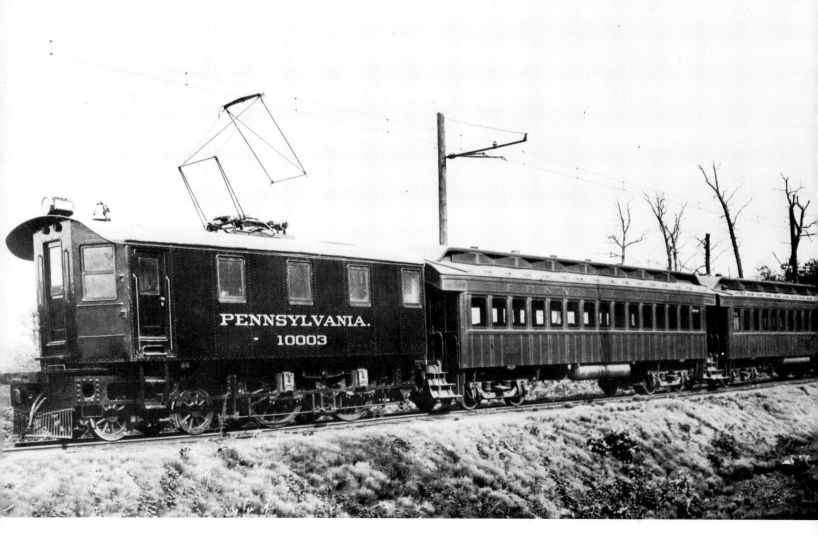

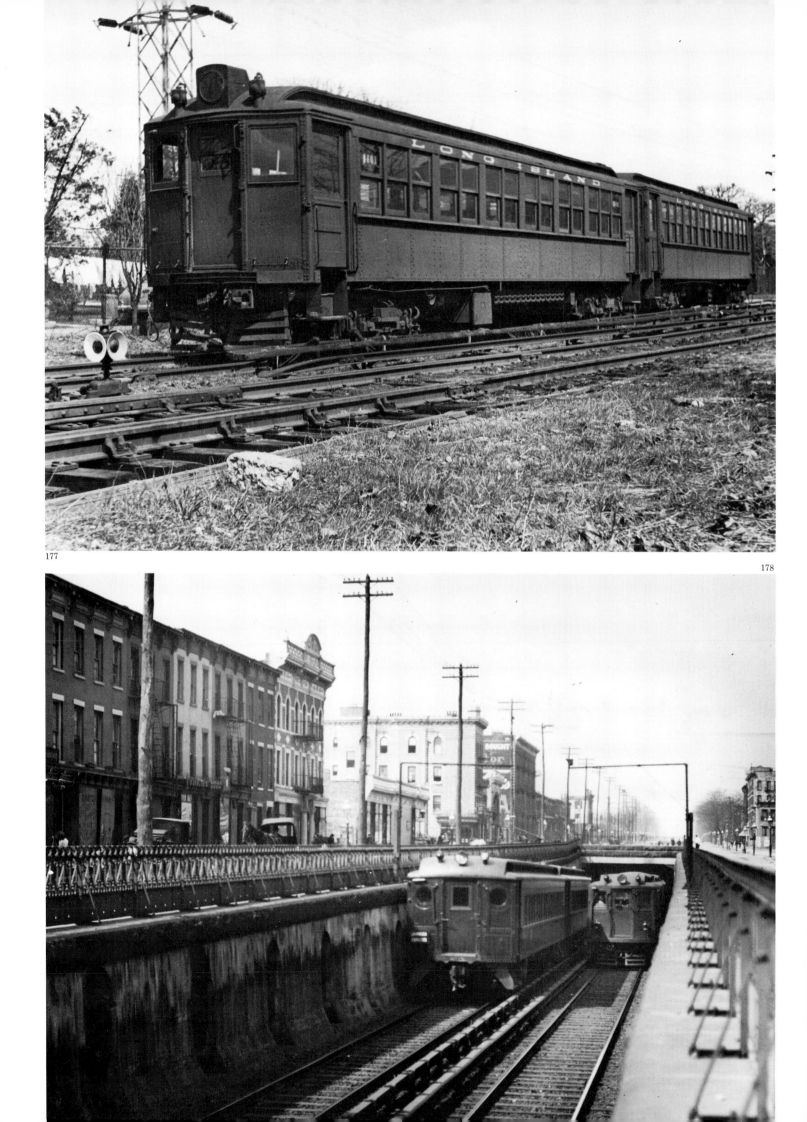

177. Electric shuttle train, Mitchel Field, April 2, 1949. Once the rapid-transit service along the Atlantic Branch to Brooklyn was eliminated by tunneling the tracks under Atlantic Avenue, most of the MP-41s became redundant, being scrapped in the 1940s. Several of them survived in regular service until 1950, forming the two-car shuttle train that ran from Country Life Press station in Garden City to the Air Force base at Mitchel Field. Originally this run had been held down by third-rail-operated trolley cars. When the MP-41s were retired, the larger MP-54s took over; shortly afterward, the service was abandoned. *(Photo by W. D. Slade; Art Huneke collection.)*

178. MP-54 and MP-41 trains at Stone Avenue, Brooklyn, 1909. Taken during what was probably a test run of the brand-new MP-54 coaches, this photo shows the tunnel portal at Stone Avenue (now Eastern Parkway) in Brooklyn, part of the 1905 upgrading of the line. Here, a much smaller train of MP-41 cars (at the right) passes a pair of MP-54s with their distinctive "owl-eye" front windows that were to become a symbol of the Long Island Rail Road for the next sixty years. *(Photo by Hal B. Fullerton; author's collection.)*

179. Crowded conditions at Bellmore, 1946. The extensive electrification of the west end of the Long Island Rail Road in the first quarter of the twentieth century helped to triple the business of the company and vastly increased the population of Queens and Nassau Counties. The consequent traffic congestion at the many grade crossings ever more frequently resulted in long delays and accidents. Impatient motorists ignored warning devices, and pedestrians became victims of "second train" accidents (crossing the tracks right behind a train, only to be struck by another train going the other way on the adjoining track). By the late 1920s, many towns along the L.I.R.R. began calling for grade-crossing-elimination projects; by the 1930s, a grand plan was instituted, calling for the raising of the railroad's Montauk Branch through all of Nassau and western Suffolk Counties. The project took a half-century to complete. Elsewhere on the railroad—notably at Mineola—the grade-crossing problems continue. Here, a westbound train of MP-54 cars has left Bellmore, and a crowd of pedestrians and automobiles waits for the raising of the hand-operated gates at Bellmore Avenue on a winter's day in 1946—a full twenty-five years before the railroad was to be elevated in this section. *(Photo by J. Burt; author's collection.)*

180

180. Quiet night at Port Washington, April 26, 1953. The heavily patronized stations within the commuting region of the L.I.R.R. grow strangely silent once the evening rush hour is past. In the terminals, such as here at Port Washington, rows of trains are laid up, their myriad of lights casting crosshatched shadows through their windows onto the deserted platforms. While this train will make a run to Penn Station in the wee hours after midnight—carrying but two or three passengers in each car—the trains on the adjoining tracks will not be leaving until morning, when thousands of commuters will ride them to their daily jobs. *(Photo by Robert Viken and Richard B. Wettereau.)*

181. An electric car of multiple functions, Babylon, ca. 1947. While most L.I.R.R. electric cars only carried passengers, some were combination cars (commonly called "combines"), which also had baggage compartments. Others were purely baggage cars and some were Railway Post Office (R.P.O.) cars. One class of multiple-unit electric cars consisted of jacks-of-all-trades, as this car, at Higbie Lane, Babylon, illustrates. Being a motor car (many electrics were trailers, without motors), it had a control cab at each end. Sandwiched between the baggage section at right and the passenger area at left (which seated approximately twenty-eight) was a small mail compartment. Although only about twelve feet long, the mail section was a bona fide R.P.O., with a mail slot in the side of the car where anyone could post letters, which were cancelled and sorted in the car. *(Photo by Ed Minden.)*

182. Clerestory-roof car interior, October 19, 1936. Old-time commuters will probably not-so-fondly recall the Spartan interiors of the 1908-design MP-54 electrics which they rode to work

as late as 1972. As built, they appeared much as in this photograph, with "walk-over" (reversible) cane-covered seats, chandelier-style center lamps and double sliding end doors, which were always left open on cold winter nights by passengers seeking out the smoking car. In the 1930s and 1940s the interiors of the cars were painted a pleasant cream and green, matching the color scheme of most of the old wooden station exteriors. In the 1950s, many of these cars were modernized with "three and two" seating, replacing the original "two and two" and moving the aisle off-center. The rattan seat covering was replaced with oilcloth, and vinyl tiles covered the composite floors. The interiors were repainted in gray and white, and fans were installed in some cars, as well as bus-type lighting with translucent white glass and clear center lenses. *(Photo by F. J. Weber; author's collection.)*

183. Round-roof car interior, 1950s. The MP-54 electric cars and the P-54 steam cars were very similar in design and came in two configurations, clerestory (or "railroad roof") and arch roof (or "round roof"). The number in the class designation referred to the length of the passenger compartment, not including the end vestibules—in this case, fifty-four feet. So alike were all types of these cars that, as electrifications expanded, many steam cars were converted for electric use and, occasionally, the reverse occurred. Here, commuters are unfolding the evening-edition *New York World-Telegram* as they await the departure of their train at Jamaica on a winter evening. Lacking the side ventilation of clerestory roofs, the arch-roof cars had square ventilators in the center of the ceiling, which provided for air circulation. *(Photo by Ron Ziel.)*

184. Into the East River tunnel, Long Island City, ca. 1955.
Realizing that the future population growth of Long Island would
require a capacity of train movements through the tunnels that
could not be predicted, the Pennsylvania Railroad had the
incredible foresight to initially build four tubes—rather than just
two—beneath the East River. Although the L.I.R.R. paid rental
on only two of the tubes, it had the use of all four during rush
hours. Even during the peak years of railway operations, during
the 1920s and through World War II, when the Pennsy itself
brought hundreds of daily trains into Penn Station from the west
and had to send them over to the Sunnyside Yard for maintenance
and storage, the tunnel facilities were never overtaxed. In recent
decades, Sunnyside, once billed as "the world's largest passenger-
car yard," has been reduced to a fraction of its peak size and Long
Island–bound trains exercise virtual free rein over the four bores.
On these high-use tracks, the third rail provides power for Long
Island multiple-unit cars, while the overhead catenary carries
electricity for Pennsy locomotives. Now Amtrak owns the vast
Pennsylvania Railroad facilities through the region known as the
Northeast Corridor. *(Photo by Irving Solomon.)*

185. Electric train gets a bath, ca. 1950. When tens of thousands
of passenger cars sped over America's railroads, serious efforts
were made to keep them clean, often utilizing laborers with
buckets of soapy water and ten-foot-long-handle brushes. In large
terminals and on systems like the Long Island, where passenger
service was extensive, automatic car washers were used. With tall
revolving brushes, jets of detergent and water were sprayed on
the cars as they slowly rolled through—a technique later copied by
similar services for autos. Here, an MP-54 gets a scrubbing at one
of several carwash facilities operated by the L.I.R.R. *(Author's
collection.)*

186. Steam and electric action at Jamaica, ca. 1949. While a
Montauk-bound train pulled by a leased Pennsy K-4s steam
engine passes Hall Tower in the background, after having left
track eight, an electric mail train arrives on track one at Jamaica
station in the foreground. Even at this late date, the L.I.R.R.
carried so much mail that it often ran entire trainloads of it into
New York. A little over fifteen years later, the railroad lost its last
mail contract and now mail trucks have joined trucks loaded with
potatoes to clog the Long Island Expressway with cargo that once
rode—and should still ride—the rails. *(Photo by Robert B. Morgan;
author's collection.)*

187. Result of head-on collision at Port Washington, August 3, 1946. Considering the hundreds of trains operated by the L.I.R.R. in its normal daily course of operations, its safety record has actually been very good, despite several catastrophic wrecks. One that claimed no passenger lives, because the train was empty at the time, occurred in Port Washington in the summer of 1946, when a DD-1 electric engine and an MP-54 had a right-of-way dispute which neither won. Car no. 1432 is shown back at Morris Park after the DD-1 had been removed. On the adjoining tracks, forty-one-year-old MP-41s, their window glass and other usable parts removed, await the scrappers' torches. *(Collection of Art Huneke.)*

188. Deadly carelessness at Rockville Centre, February 19, 1950. After the Pennsylvania Railroad disavowed the debts of its "stepchild" L.I.R.R. in 1949 and let the hapless line slide into bankruptcy, the morale of the work force plummeted. It was the era before automatic speed control and other "fail-safe" devices greatly reduced the chance of accidents caused by human error, and the elimination of grade crossings, etc., at Rockville Centre was already under way. Because of tight clearances, the two temporary tracks had to overlap in a gantlet section. The motorman of one train sped right through a stop signal, and an oncoming train split the lead car of his train lengthwise right down the middle, killing thirty-three passengers inside. The motorman, later tried for manslaughter, was uninjured, though trapped in his cab, which was the only part of the front of the car to escape damage. Many passengers on that side of the car were unscathed, while people sitting two feet away across the aisle were mangled beyond recognition, a sobering example of capricious fate. The following August, the Huntington station wreck (see photo no. 141, above) injured scores of passengers, and on Thanksgiving Eve eighty-five died in a rear-end collision between two M.U. trains at Richmond Hill. It was these events in the calamitous year of 1950 that led to court-imposed safety systems and the eventual takeover of the Long Island Rail Road by the State of New York. *(Photo by F. J. Weber; author's collection.)*

189. DD-1 electric locomotive, Jamaica, ca. 1948. Even before the Pennsylvania Railroad electrified its lines between New York and Washington, D.C., and west to Harrisburg in the 1930s, the DD-1s were being replaced by more modern motive power. So the Long Island began buying the original electrics, using them to haul steam trains to Jamaica and in electrified-territory freight service. By 1944, the L.I.R.R. had acquired more than two-thirds of the boxy locomotives. Instead of being powered by axle-mounted traction motors as was the case with contemporary trolley cars and still is, to this day, with modern diesel and electric engines, the DD-1 employed the Quill-drive principle. Huge motors were installed in the car bodies, with driving rods leading to a flywheel. Connecting rods powered the sixty-eight-inch driving wheels, giving the DD-1 the appearance of a steam locomotive whose boiler was completely enclosed by the cab. The DD-1 was actually two locomotives semipermanently coupled back-to-back, and the pair of units could not be operated separately. *(Photo by Robert B. Morgan; author's collection.)*

190. Electric-powered freight, Rockville Centre, ca. 1948. With the acquisition of the DD-1 fleet, the Long Island electrified many industrial sidings, enabling it to remove sooty steam engines from working in what were often residential areas. The Creedmoor Branch is a case in point: it ran right past many densely packed houses, where the smoke and noise of steam invariably riled the residents. But a 650-volt exposed third rail just a few feet from where little children played was even less desirable, so the railroad ran the DD-1s on that spur only late at night, turning off the power in daylight, when the children were about. By the mid-1940s the Creedmoor Branch reverted back to steam and the disused third rail became enveloped in rust and weeds. The Long Island scrapped all of its DD-1s by 1952, but the Pennsylvania preserved one for historical purposes. *(Photo by Ed Minden.)*

191. Rare electric switch engines, Bay Ridge, October 1952. The use of electric switch engines anywhere in the world is rare indeed, owing to the high cost of electrifying low-use sidings and interchange and engine-servicing tracks. Because of its intense passenger-train activity, the Pennsy found it economical and good public relations to utilize electric shunters at Sunnyside and in the Philadelphia yards. By the mid-1920s, when the overhead catenary was strung down the Bay Ridge Branch, the Long Island also found that replacing steam with "juice" engines on that heavily residential line would be advantageous. The L.I.R.R. did the logical thing, ordering fourteen little B-3 six-wheel "goats," which were virtually identical with parent Pennsy's. Built in 1926 at the Pennsylvania's Juniata Shops in Altoona, they worked for nearly three decades, coincidentally being retired at the same time as the last steam engines. The ones owned by the P.R.R. were used for another twenty years and, as with the DD-1, the Pennsy wisely preserved one. (Its historical collection is now displayed at the Pennsylvania State Railroad Museum at Strasburg.) *(Photo by F. G. Zahn.)*

L.I.R.R. keystone logo (1920s–1950s).

192. Electric shop switcher, Morris Park, ca. 1949. Shop switchers, be they steam, diesel or electric, have always been diminutive affairs. Rarely do they have to drag around more than one dead engine or car at a time, so they need not be powerful or fast. They must, however, be as short as possible, in order to fit onto a turntable or transfer table with whatever they happen to be moving around. The L.I.R.R. has operated several electric shop engines, one being a homemade job that was created by the simple expedient of mounting a cab, controls and couplers on an M.U. truck. No. 320, shown here, was more sophisticated; it was built by Baldwin and equipped by Westinghouse in 1927 and worked the Morris Park Shops until 1958. All shop engines are now small diesels. *(Photo by James V. Osborne; author's collection.)*

193. L.I.R.R. trolley car, Philadelphia, 1898. Perhaps the most renowned of trolley-car builders in America was the J. G. Brill Company of Philadelphia. When the L.I.R.R. began taking over horsecar lines in the 1890s, as well as building its own trolley routes as feeders between large villages and stations that were sometimes several miles away, it turned to Brill for rolling stock. Handsome open cars, such as no. E6, shown here, were used only during the summer months in the Rockaways and on the Ocean Electric Line; as summer business grew further east, they also ran on the Huntington Electric Railroad, between Halesite and Amityville. In the era before modern air-conditioning was developed to hermetically seal passengers inside railroad and rapid-transit cars, patrons were cooled by fresh breezes wafting through the completely open cars. *(Collection of Jeffrey Winslow.)*

194. Battery car, West Hempstead Branch, Mineola, 1923. Running the West Hempstead Branch shuttle train in Nassau and the Bushwick Branch in Brooklyn with a steam engine and a lone wooden coach was an expensive endeavor, requiring at least three crewmen, so, in the early teens, the railroad began using cars powered by chargeable storage batteries. Later on, they were equipped with third-rail pick-up shoes, enabling them to run greater distances. The development of gasoline-powered railcars and gas-electric cars enabled the company to utilize equipment that was larger, heavier and faster—and was not limited by battery time—so the battery cars were retired in the mid-1920s, while the gasoline cars continued to hold down the timetables on the Wading River and Sag Harbor Branches until the two lines were abandoned in the late 1930s. *(Photo by James V. Osborne; author's collection.)*

CHAPTER TWELVE

Leased Pennsylvania Railroad Locomotives

195

195. Little goat from the Keystone State, Morris Park, August 26, 1936. The mighty Pennsylvania Railroad, in its heyday early in this century, accounted for about fifteen percent of track-miles operated in the United States; it also ran about twenty percent of all passenger-miles and nearly as much of freight-miles and—in the early 1920s—owned about twelve percent of all locomotives (more than 7,500). What with the effects of seasonal variations and a changing economic climate, plus the Pennsy's electrification in the Northeast in the 1930s, there was always a surplus of steam locomotives. So, rather than have the Long Island invest heavily in new engines, the P.R.R. was happy to lease motive power at rates that ran from $40 to $100 per day per engine. For the L.I.R.R., it meant having all the engines it needed at low short-term rates. For the Pennsy, the arrangement let it send over a lot of old junkers and derelicts that had to be repaired (at the lessee's expense). Also, the Penn often supplied locomotives that were ready for retirement, so they were sent to Long Island for a few months, to run out their last miles and earn the P.R.R. a few final dollars in rental fees. The smallest of the leased engines were the B-8-class six-wheel switchers, built just after the turn of the century. Here, no. 2504 shuffles past Dunton Tower at the east end of the Morris Park engine terminal, on the way to a switching assignment. *(Photo by Edward L. May.)*

196. The Patchogue Scoot at its namesake station, ca. 1944. Viewed from "PD" Tower at South Ocean Avenue, the local shuttle train from Babylon has just arrived, its quartet of "ping-pong" coaches powered by leased Pennsy 4-4-2 no. 3005. Although being retired by the P.R.R. and dispatched quickly to scrap yards for the steel-starved war effort, these little E-3sd and the similar E-7s Atlantics were ideally suited for hauling the "Scoot"—a train whose consist seldom topped 200 tons in weight. For reasons long lost in history, local shuttle trains have always been called "Scoot" by L.I.R.R. men. Even four decades into the diesel era, the Babylon–Patchogue local is still known as the "Patchogue Scoot." The brick express house in the foreground and the 1888 station behind it, as well as the watering column at right, are long gone,

but the Patchogue Scoot continues its daily round-trips to Babylon. *(Collection of F. G. Zahn.)*

197. The "Lindbergh Engine" at Greenport, August 14, 1938. To be fair to the Pennsylvania Railroad, it must be noted that while it often sent locomotives that were in scandalous mechanical condition to Long Island, it also leased some of the finest specimens on the roster. Fully one-third of the eighty-three E-6s 4-4-2s built between 1910 and 1914 were operated on the L.I.R.R. from 1935 to 1949, including what was perhaps the most famous of the 25,000 steam engines the Pennsy owned over a 110-year period: E-6s no. 460. Her stint on Long Island during the late 1930s was appropriate, for when Charles A. Lindbergh took off from Long Island on a foggy morning in May 1927, nobody could have guessed the role that the big 4-4-2 would later play in a postscript to that epic first solo nonstop trans-Atlantic flight. In the days before television brought the news of the day into almost every living room in America, newsreel films, shown in local theaters, attracted vast crowds after a major event occurred. So it was that, when Lindbergh returned from Paris, he received a tumultuous reception by President Calvin Coolidge, Congress and all of Washington, D.C. Thousands of people waited at Times Square theaters to see the newsreels from the nation's capital, as the three competing companies raced their films to New York. Two of the firms loaded their undeveloped films onto airplanes and flew them up. The third—the International News Reel Company—contracted with the Pennsylvania Railroad to supply a locomotive, a baggage car–turned–darkroom and a coach to carry its films, which were developed and printed en route. Although the newsreel footage carried by the airplanes arrived in New York first, the record run of no. 460 (216 miles in 175 minutes at speeds up to 115 miles per hour) delivered the developed films a full hour ahead of the competition, whose reels of film were still being processed at labs in Long Island City. No. 460, for the rest of her career affectionately known as "the engine that beat the airplanes," was the only E-6s to be preserved; it can be visited at the Pennsylvania State Railroad Museum. *(Photo by Charles B. Chaney; Smithsonian Institution.)*

198

199

200

198. The engine terminal at Patchogue, 1941. Since a number of commuter trains terminated at Patchogue, as well as the "Scoot" trains from Babylon and a local freight, engine-servicing facilities were a necessity in steam days. At one time there was even an engine house, but in 1941—just a decade before total dieselization of the Montauk Branch—the turntable and coaling crane were still very actively supporting the locomotives that called at Patchogue. Here, a G-5s, E-6s no. 1287, an older E-class 4-4-2 and another E-6s percolate on the terminal tracks between runs. *(Photo by R. M. Emery; author's collection.)*

199. Westbound "Fish Train," Shinnecock Canal, 1940. The legendary speed runs of the Fisherman's Specials to Montauk were usually powered by eighty-inch-driving-wheel E-6s engines in the 1930s and 1940s. Racing out of Jamaica before dawn, they arrived at Montauk in time to fill the party boats and returned in the late afternoon. A stop was also made at a short cinder platform, just east of the Shinnecock Bridge, where anglers went out on the Hampton Bays fishing boats. Here, an unknown photographer caught no. 1611 as she paused to board fishermen who had returned from a day of deep-sea angling south of Shinnecock Inlet. *(Author's collection.)*

200. Steam-electric race, Union Hall Street, September 1, 1947. Heading east from Jamaica station, two trains often raced (intentionally or not) as they gained momentum speeding their passengers to their destinations. The Union Hall Street stop, less than a mile from Jamaica station, was a favorite spot to view the action as the engineers of a pair of steam locomotives, or a steam engineer and electric motorman, accelerated their trains. Although management frowned on the practice, hotshot engineers actually did race, and a pair of trains that had been approaching forty m.p.h. at Union Hall Street might have been doing seventy-five by Queens Village. Here, Pennsy E-6s no. 1321 races neck and neck with an MP-54 electric train, the engineer of the steamer leaning out of his cab in the traditional manner. *(Photo by W. D. Slade; Art Huneke collection.)*

201. Dropping a semaphore blade at Floral Park, 1947. Thundering past "Park" Tower at Floral Park at better than sixty miles per hour on a clear cold winter's day, no. 1564 whips up the powdery snow on her eastward dash. The fleecy plume of exhaust steam from the stack is mixed with just a bit of gray smoke in the frigid air. The blade of the semaphore signal is already dropping to the stop position, with the engine barely past. The L.I.R.R. once operated hundreds of semaphores; they went the way of wooden coaches and steam locomotives by the mid-1960s, when the last ones were replaced by the circular position-light signals of more modern design. *(Photo by Harry J. Trede; author's collection.)*

Leased Pennsylvania Railroad Locomotives 135

202. Light Pacific in an Atlantic snow storm, East Hampton, January 1942. The most popular wheel arrangement for passenger locomotives in the 1900s was the 4–6–2, named the Pacific type. The Long Island Rail Road never owned a Pacific, but it leased at least eighty-five of them from the Pennsy between 1931 and 1951, including no. 3570, seen here, a K-2s of 1910-era vintage. This medium-size 4–6–2 makes short work of a heavy snowfall as it pauses briefly at Newtown Lane, East Hampton, before sprinting onward to Amagansett and Montauk. *(Photo by David Elliot.)*

203. Debut of the great K-4s on Long Island, Mineola, June 27, 1931. One of the most famed and successful of locomotive designs in all of American railroad history was the K-4s 4–6–2 Pacific passenger steam engine of the Pennsylvania. The prototype was built in 1914 and, after extensive testing, the P.R.R. ordered 424 additional ones between 1917 and 1927. Big, rugged and simply straightforward in design and performance, the powerful eighty-inch-driving-wheel 4–6–2 was the backbone of the Pennsy's "Great Steel Fleet" passenger power for more than three decades, its service life spanning forty-three years. Through the 1920s, 1930s and 1940s—including the World War II era with its crushing work pace—the K-4s powered the grandest of the P.R.R. named trains, including the Broadway Limited, the "Spirit of St. Louis," the Congressional, the Liberty Limited, the Trail Blazer, the

Jeffersonian, the New Yorker and the Cincinnatian, as well as shorter-run, local and lowly commuter trains. With the drop in patronage during the Depression, followed by the electrification of the P.R.R.'s eastern reaches, the Pennsy was able to spare a few K-4s engines for powering the heavy and fast "Straw Hat Limiteds" to the Hamptons and Montauk during the summer season. They first ran on Long Island in late June of 1931, and this photo of train no. 20, the Cannon Ball, thundering through Mineola on June 27, is believed to have been taken on the first day of K-4s running on the L.I.R.R. In sending the K-4s engines to the Long Island (as many as thirteen at one time) the Pennsy did much to clear itself of the charge that it only provided decrepit, obsolete junkers to its subsidiary. *(Photo by Charles B. Chaney; Smithsonian Institution.)*

204. Pennsy Pacific leaving Jamaica, October 4, 1947. Although the K-4s engines were initially sent to Long Island for summer service, as early as 1935 they were remaining year-round. The big Pacifics worked constantly on the L.I.R.R. until October 1951, when the last four were returned to the Pennsy, to run out their final years in New Jersey commuter service; the last was finally retired in 1957. Long Island enginemen fondly recall the big engines for their reliability, responsiveness and speed. *(Photo by George Hamcke.)*

202

Leased Pennsylvania Railroad Locomotives   *137*

205. Rounding Yaphank curve, 1949. Once more of the K-4s locomotives became available to the Long Island Rail Road, the motive-power superintendent eagerly assigned them to the heaviest Greenport trains and the most demanding of Port Jefferson runs, as well as Montauk jobs. In the years following World War II, some high P.R.R. officials decided that, in order to make maintaining engines slightly more convenient, the positions of the headlight and electrical generator should be reversed. The result of this "face-lifting" or "beauty treatment"—as railroaders called it—was an aesthetic calamity, as no. 5396, seen here racing around Yaphank curve on the Main Line, woefully illustrates. *(Photo by Robert B. Morgan; author's collection.)*

206. Mechanical delay at Riverhead, 1948. One day, as no. 7270 came to a halt at Riverhead station, her air pump jammed, and, with no air, the brakes were locked. While the passengers—including a soldier, seen here contemplating the pilot wheels—milled about the platform for two hours, a local plumber on a ladder worked to repair the recalcitrant compressor. His ultimate success enabled the K-4s once more to eat up the miles through the pine barrens along the Main Line in central Suffolk County. *(Photo by Robert B. Morgan; author's collection.)*

207. Greenport-bound on a bleak winter's day, Central Islip, March 6, 1949. In addition to the "face-lifting" of the headlight, which included the addition of an unsightly servicing platform beneath the smokebox door, the K-4s and some other Pennsy engines were also fitted with a heavy solid steel pilot and a hinged drop-coupler, which proved to be a practical improvement. Often in grade-crossing accidents, a highway vehicle would be impaled on the coupler; the new arrangement deflected such obstacles as busses, Buicks and bovines! K-4s no. 1554 models the new look as she speeds an eleven-car Greenport-bound train toward Ronkonkoma. Mercifully, no Long Island–owned engines ever were subjected to the front-end beauty treatment. *(Photo by John Krause; author's collection.)*

208. Laying down the soot, Stony Brook, 1950. In a classic scene of branch-line railroading, no. 3655—one of the last four of a total of seventy-one K-4s engines known to have run on the L.I.R.R.—erupts in a veritable miasma of soft-coal smoke at a relatively remote spot along the Port Jefferson line. The heavy smoke had been prearranged by the photographer prior to the departure of the train from Port Jefferson, for the dramatic photographic effect. Nowadays, "smoke arrangements" for the benefit of the cameras are commonplace when preserved locomotives are making their occasional runs, but, back in the regular-service days of 1950, the practice was rare indeed. *(Photo by John Krause; author's collection.)*

CHAPTER THIRTEEN

Internal-Combustion Power

209. Brill gas car, Sag Harbor, July 5, 1935. Even after the Long Island Rail Road began to electrify in earnest, no knowledgeable observers ever doubted that the role of steam in the motive-power affairs of the company would remain preeminent. On the other hand, visionary railroad officials, relying more on hope than practicality, predicted the eventual total electrification of the railroad as late as World War II, sincerely believing that it would greatly benefit the region. Of course, the problem was (and remains) that it could be *too* good; running third rail all the way to Greenport and Montauk would put those areas within commuting distance of Manhattan, which would rapidly accelerate the development of the last pristine rural sections of Long Island and destroy their bucolic beauty, not to mention the delicate natural balance. Traction motors did eventually do steam in, but in the form of diesel generators supplying the electric current—not power substations and third rail. The earliest replacement of steam came in 1927, when the low-utilization branches between Port Jefferson and Wading River, and between Bridgehampton and Sag Harbor, began being served by gasoline-powered railcars. (In fact, the first diesel had arrived in 1925—two years earlier—but the units did not actually supersede steam on any particular branch.) Here, car no. 1134, built by the J. G. Brill Company (renowned for the construction of trolley cars), is shown alongside Sag Harbor station, less than four years before the branch was abandoned. The car was later sold to the Atlantic & Western Railroad of Sanford, North Carolina, and, in an advanced state of decay, it survives today in Ohio. *(Photo by William J. Rugen; Art Huneke collection.)*

210. Pennsy gas-electric, Morris Park, ca. 1935. Much larger than the Brill cars, the gas-electrics worked more on the diesel principle, with the power plant generating electricity to run traction motors. P.R.R. no. 4670, shown riding the transfer table at the Morris Park Shops, was one of a pair leased by the L.I.R.R. during the Depression, when it frequently held down main-line schedules. Unlike the direct-drive Brill cars, the powerful gas-electrics could pull one or two other cars. It is easy to understand how one of these economical cars could save the railroad a tidy sum of money when it replaced a steam locomotive and two coaches and their larger crew. *(Art Huneke collection.)*

211. The first "oil-electric" locomotive, Morris Park, ca. 1948. Costing $100,000—a phenomenal sum in 1925, when the L.I.R.R. was purchasing G-5s steam passenger engines for less than one-third the price—this steel box was one of the most important locomotives in the history of railroading. As the world's first diesel-electric to be placed in main-line service, no. 401 was the pioneer machine that ultimately will have brought about the global demise of the steam locomotive, a phenomenon that began in the United States just before World War II and will end, no doubt, in China and India early in the twenty-first century. Originally called "oil-electrics," the first diesels proved their mettle over steam-powered switch engines, but it would be another decade before they were perfected to seriously challenge modern steam in main-line service. Although it worked in switching service until 1951, by which time its historical value should have been greatly appreciated, this important locomotive was not preserved. *(Photo by Robert B. Morgan; author's collection.)*

209

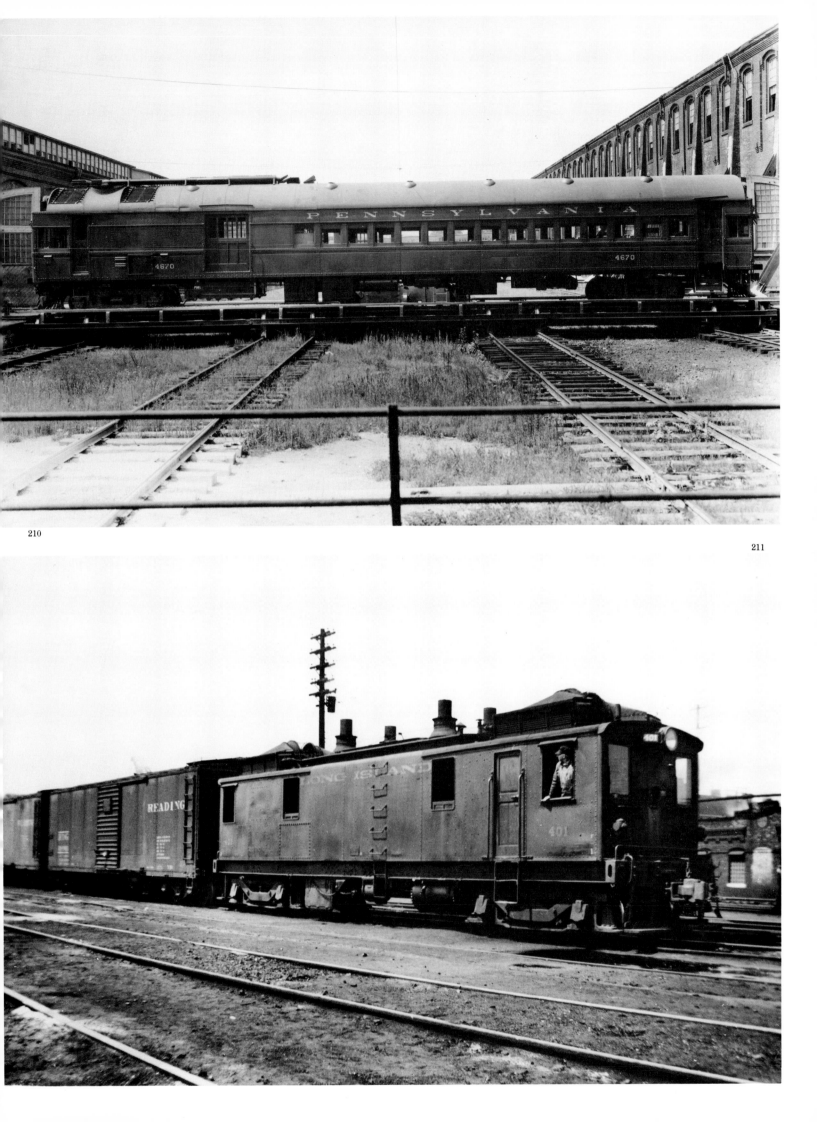

212

212. The second no. 402, Morris Park, ca. 1948. The first no. 402, constructed by trolley-and-gas-car builder Brill in 1926, was a gasoline-powered, traction-motored locomotive that lasted only a few weeks before the L.I.R.R. apparently invoked the warranty, returning it for a number of defects. The second no. 402, seen here, was built by Ingersoll-Rand, whose successful no. 401 made the railroad stick with proven competence. Although very similar to its predecessor, the 402, built in 1928, managed to perform equally well with a configuration a full six feet shorter. It survived in local switching service until 1951, having led a useful life that equaled that—almost to the month—of five of the G-5s engines that had also been built in 1928 and were retired in the latter half of 1951! *(Photo by Robert B. Morgan; author's collection.)*

213. "Ike" and "Mike" were separable, Flushing Meadow, 1940. Diesels nos. 403A and 403B were built as a single, semipermanently coupled locomotive composed of two units, each with its own 330-horsepower engine, so when the railroad later decided to separate them, it just took a few modifications to do so. Built by Baldwin and equipped with Westinghouse electrical gear, they switched the factory sidings of the West End of Long Island (mostly in Brooklyn) until their separate retirements toward the end of the Second World War. Nicknamed "Ike" and "Mike" by the men who ran them, the little four-wheel units did not last as long as their larger pioneer diesel compatriots, but were remarkably successful, nevertheless, for such early examples of a whole new concept in technology. Here, no. 403B shunts gondola cars at the 1939 World's Fair site in the Borough of Queens. The later generation of sleek, streamlined diesels and the bland, stubby freight haulers of today all can trace their lineage back to the Long Island's square box-cabs of the 1920s. *(Photo by Jeffrey Winslow.)*

214. Steam-to-diesel transition, Oyster Bay, May 24, 1953. The L.I.R.R. began ordering diesels to replace steam power in 1948, and within just seven years it went off the coal standard for good. In that period of transition, there were many opportunities to see the lions and the lambs lying down together—especially during weekend layovers—at Morris Park, Oyster Bay, Port Jefferson and Ronkonkoma. Here, a 1925 G-5s steamer, no. 24, has symbolically already "taken the back seat" to no. 462, a 1,000-horsepower road diesel built by the American Locomotive Company (ALCO) at the outset of the dieselization program in 1948. *(Photo by Robert Viken and Richard B. Wettereau.)*

215. Farewell to steam, Hicksville, June 5, 1955. With total dieselization of the L.I.R.R.'s nonelectrified operations made imminent by the pending arrival of ten 1,600-horsepower ALCO RS-3's in September 1955, several final steam excursions were operated by the railroad. On June 5th, G-5s no. 39 pulled the last steam-powered passenger train ever to run to Greenport, the terminal of the original Main Line, closing out a tradition that had gone on for 111 years. When the train paused at Hicksville, hundreds of passengers poured off the ten-car special to admire and photograph the old ten-wheeler at the head end. No. 39 and no. 35 were the only L.I.R.R.-owned steam engines to be preserved. Almost thirty-five years after this photo was taken, the 39 is slowly being completely renovated in the railroad yard in Riverhead, from where it will eventually pull steam-powered excursion trains along the old Main Line and, ultimately, other branches as well. *(Photo by George E. Votava.)*

217

218

216. The last steam run, Bay Ridge, October 16, 1955. By early in October, the new RS-3 diesels were in service, and the last commuter trains to go out behind steam were slated to leave Oyster Bay the morning of October 10. Two days earlier, on a rainy Saturday, nos. 35 and 39, each pulling a brand-new coach loaded with Boy Scouts, met at Hicksville for official "end-of-steam" ceremonies. Then, RS-3 no. 1556 was coupled behind no. 39's coach and no. 1555 behind that of no. 35, returning the cars to Jamaica and Riverhead, respectively. On Sunday, October 16, no. 35 was fired up one last time, to pull a railfan extra down the Bay Ridge Branch, then out to Babylon and up to Port Jefferson, returning to Jamaica. This picture, taken beneath a bridge on the Bay Ridge leg of the trip, symbolizes the demise of steam, as the last active Long Island steamer heads into the gloom and darkness of oblivion. Despite the great success of the last steam excursions and the publicity bent of his administration, railroad President Thomas M. Goodfellow ignored the pleas of the public and the advice of his own officials to retain a pair of the old engines for excursions. Nos. 35 and 39 were sent to static display sites (the 35 at Salisbury Park, the 39 to The Museums at Stony Brook) where they remained for nearly a quarter of a century. Then, under separate agreements, each was brought back to railroad property to be restored to operation. The 35 project later failed and no. 39, moved to Riverhead in 1980, suffered owing to the incompetence of the contractor who was to rebuild and operate it. Despite a total lack of support from the MTA and virtually no cooperation from L.I.R.R. management, scores of volunteers continue to work on no. 39 outdoors, fired by the dream of eventually returning her to the high iron. *(Photo by Bill Finn; author's collection.)*

217. End of the line for no. 116, Modena, Pennsylvania, July 1952. L.I.R.R. engines 35 and 39 were fortunate, every other steam locomotive ever owned by the railroad having been cut up for scrap. Here, H-10s no. 116 awaits the acetylene torches at the Luria Brothers Scrapyard at Modena, Pennsylvania. Within weeks, she was cut up and her steel reclaimed, to be made into 1953 Fords, hairpins or Patton tanks for the Korean front. *(Harold K. Vollrath collection.)*

218. The diesel triumphant, Babylon, August 23, 1952. By the end of 1951, the Montauk Branch was completely dieselized and steam only made rare appearances on work trains or as emergency replacement power for a failed diesel. Here a train of MP-54 multiple-unit cars waits at the high-level wooden platform at Babylon, while a diesel rolls through with a local freight. *(Photo by W. D. Slade; Art Huneke collection.)*

219. Fairbanks-Morse diesel leaving Oyster Bay, ca. 1953. On a winter's day, no. 1504 rolls a train of four light "ping-pong" coaches out of the yard and down the Oyster Bay Branch in the transition era when steam still ran on these tracks. Railroad men liked the F-M diesels, which only lasted about thirteen years, before being retired in favor of a fleet of ALCO C-420s. When the ALCOs were retired in the late 1970s, the L.I.R.R. acquired its fourth generation of road diesels—running through three generations in the normal span of one steam generation! *(Photo by John Krause; author's collection.)*

219

220. C-Liner at Smithtown, ca. 1952. The L.I.R.R. ordered a quartet of 2,400-horsepower Fairbanks-Morse diesels specifically to replace the last four leased Pennsylvania Railroad K-4s Pacific steam engines. When the F-M "C-Liners" arrived, in the early autumn of 1951, the 4-6-2s were promptly returned to their owner. In their two-tone gray paint scheme, with bright red pilots and high shaded numerals, the new "growlers" presented a sleek, streamlined image that went with the "new look" so ardently sought by the management of the L.I.R.R., as the railroad recovered from the disastrous wrecks of 1950 and the bankruptcy into which it had been thrust by the Pennsy. *(Photo by John Krause; author's collection.)*

221. The new order, Stony Brook, 1955. In the spring of 1955, the railroad received an order of new air-conditioned coaches that were an incredible luxury to commuters accustomed to bouncing to work in old clunkers that dated back to the camelback era. The following winter, with steam finally gone from the L.I.R.R., a westbound C-Liner pulled a train composed of an old combine and a half-dozen of the new coaches into Stony Brook station. The picturesque semaphore, another symbol of the steam era, had but a year or two to go as well. Once seen at almost every station, these manually operated train-order signals were removed in the late 1950s. Only two were saved, the one in this photo now owned by the author of this volume. *(Photo by John Krause; author's collection.)*

222. Queens of the diesel reign, Port Jefferson, 1955. The two major configurations of Fairbanks-Morse diesels overshadowed the more prosaic Baldwin and ALCO diesels that dominated the L.I.R.R. roster in 1955. Being more powerful, the F-M diesels were also more apt to be used on both the heaviest commuter runs and the summer season "Straw Hat Limiteds" to the Hamptons. Although often seen on passenger trains, the boxy 1500's were also used as freight haulers; the 2400's rarely—if ever—saw freight use. Just a few years earlier, this scene would have featured a K-4s 4-6-2 and an H-10s 2-8-0 or a G-5s 4-6-0. *(Photo by John Krause; author's collection.)*

223. Modernization of the old Scoot, Babylon, 1955. The local Scoot between Babylon and Patchogue was dieselized in September 1949, when the last E-6s steamers were returned to the Pennsylvania. In 1955, a pair of Budd Company Rail Diesel Cars (RDC) was bought by the L.I.R.R., and for several years they held down the Scoot timetable. Ultimately, they were given other assignments and the Scoot reverted to diesel locomotives and coaches. Although the RDCs were of practical use to the L.I.R.R., they were never duplicated on the Island. *(Photo by Irving Solomon.)*

224. Postscript I: Steam visitor at Long Island City, November 24, 1967. After twelve years had passed since the demise of steam on the Long Island Rail Road, a clamor of public support had arisen for the idea of operating steam excursions to the East End. To prove the point, the author and George H. Foster leased Black River & Western 2-8-0 no. 60 and, on November 26, 1967, ran her to Montauk, with a long train of happy passengers behind and tens of thousands of onlookers (50,000 in the western half of Suffolk County alone) along the right-of-way, cheering the doughty Consolidation onward. The L.I.R.R. float operation at Long Island City was in its last years and, though the railroad had sold its own tugs and barges a few years previously, other railways still brought their own floats in. When the Central Railroad of New Jersey delivered no. 60 and the former C.N.J. vice-president's business car, which also made the Montauk trip, the author decided to photograph the arrival. Several photos were made, including this one, printed from a five-by-seven-inch glass-plate negative, shot with the same 1909 Graflex camera that had been used by Joseph Burt, the renowned Mineola photographer. What was unknown at the time, out of several thousand floatings of steam locomotives between New Jersey and Long Island between the 1880s and 1955, none had apparently ever been photographed. This, then is the irony: a dozen years after all steam ceased on the L.I.R.R., one final move was made by float, and this move is the only one of which photos are known to exist. With the abandonment of these nautical facilities, the situation can never be repeated! *(Photo by Ron Ziel.)*

225. Postscript II: Last relics of the glory days, Quogue, June 14, 1968. The famed 1920s-era heavyweight parlor cars rolled on well into the drab and dreary era of the MTA on Long Island. This scene of train no. 22, the Cannon Ball, the last all-parlor-car train in America, could well have been taken forty-five years earlier, when a brace of high-wheeled camelbacks would have brought up the head end. *(Photo by Ron Ziel.)*

Index

Numbers refer to *pages*, not specific captions.